Mary Berry is known to millions through her regular cookery spot on Thames Television's magazine programme, *After Noon Plus*. She is a regular contributor to BBC *Woman's Hour* and often takes part in BBC and local radio phone-in programmes.

Mary Berry was for several years, cookery editor of *Ideal Home* and is now the *Home and Freezer Digest*'s cookery consultant. She is one of Britain's most popular cookery writers and has written over twenty cookery books.

Also by Mary Berry in Sphere Books:

Kitchen Wisdom

MARY BERRY

SPHERE BOOKS LIMITED
London and Sydney

First published in Great Britain by
Judy Piatkus (Publishers) Limited 1985
Copyright © 1985 Mary Berry
Published by Sphere Books Ltd 1986
30–32 Gray's Inn Road, London, WC1X 8JL

My thanks go to Debbie Woolhead who has
deciphered these tips and hints from the backs of
envelopes, scraps of paper and reams of foolscap.
Many of her own ideas have been included. I am
also very grateful to Susan Fleming who has spent
hours with us, editing this into a logical and, I
hope, practical book.

Set in Horley Old Style

Printed and bound in Great Britain by
Cox & Wyman Ltd, Reading

Contents

Introduction

In my recipes I have always tried to give extra tips which add to the success of the final result. In fact, a large proportion of the letters I receive from readers and viewers mention these tips and say how useful they are.

For it is undeniably true that most recipes state the 'obvious' – they record the bare facts and never go into the little details which can make all the difference to a less experienced cook who is preparing the dish for the first time.

I have been creating and cooking recipes for many years, and inevitably I have accumulated hundreds of tips. At the same time, I have amassed a great many ideas about how kitchens should be equipped, furnished and run. And it is this collected 'wisdom' that I would like to pass on in this book.

I have planned four kitchens now, and know exactly what I want and need. Obviously my professional needs are greater than those of the average kitchen-user, but the principles are the same, so I hope my advice about planning and types of equipment will be useful and will point you in the right direction.

The buying, storing and preparing of food are major activities central to every kitchen, and my tips should cover almost every eventuality. I have also included many topics dear to my heart, like how to slim while producing all those delicious goodies, and how to cope with the safety – and happiness – of children in the kitchen.

The other major activity in *every* kitchen is washing and cleaning, and my tips cover basic laundry, washing up (where a logical approach *can* help!) and cleaning tricky things like oven shelves (I thank the day my younger brother gave me that tip about soaking them in biological washing powder).

I hope that all these ideas, the fruit of many years of trial and error on my part, will help you solve some of your problems, or at least make them easier!

Mary Berry

Planning a kitchen

I have planned four kitchens from scratch, so I now know exactly what I want! As I spend a lot of time in the kitchen, I spent a lot of time planning it. I suggest you do the same.

How to start No one can really plan your kitchen *for* you, unless you give them a detailed brief of what you want. Think of your *own* needs first. Do you cook a lot or a little? Do you want to eat in the kitchen? Must you keep the freezer and do the washing there?

Plan it out first If you want to do it yourself, get some graph paper and note on it the exact size, shape, placement of any fixtures (windows, doors, points, pipes etc). Cut cardboard shapes to scale to represent fridge, cooker etc.

The work triangle The three most constantly used areas – the fridge, sink and cooker – and it makes sense to house them near each other. The total length of the three sides should be between 6.6 m (22 ft) and 3.6 m (12 ft).

The sink A double sink is always better than a single. One can be used for food preparation while the other is full of dirty dishes; one can also hold hot rinsing water for dishes or hand-washed clothes.

Size of sink Ideally, a sink should be big enough to take an oven shelf – probably the largest object needing washing in the average kitchen.

Floor units Good fitted kitchen units always help to sell a house – when you've finished planning one kitchen and are ready to embark on the next! Choose the best – those that need the least maintenance. Laminates show every mark, and intricate patterns or louvres are difficult to clean. Mine are of sealed dark oak which only need the occasional quick wipe.

Unit shelves Sometimes adjustable shelves and *narrower* shelves are more convenient; different height objects can be stored, and many don't need to be stored on top of or behind each other.

Working surfaces You must have one next to the cooker. They're also vital next to the sink – although you can often improvise, with a board.

Working surfaces should be practical, durable and heatproof. A good surface for both sinks and worktops is the American synthetic marble, Corian, which is tough, cool and easy to clean.

Kitchen walls Walls in a kitchen have to withstand heat, splashes and steam. Paint is the simplest, and gloss is easily washed. Tiles are tough and easy to clean. Wallpaper should be coated in spongeable vinyl, but tiles are best round the steamy cooker or sink areas.

Kitchen floors Ease of cleaning is the first consideration, with durability a close second. I now have ceramic tiles, which are dog-proof, child-proof, stain-resistant, non-slip, attractive and hard-wearing. Choose a slight pattern which won't show dirt so much. A pure white floor may *look* attractive, but needs constant attention.

Wall units Wall units are a major space saver in the kitchen, but do be sure that you can reach to the back of the highest shelf!

Cooking and eating I always like to eat in the kitchen – life is so much happier. If you have room, the kitchen is where informal family eating should take place. A door closed between the cook and the eaters is sad. If space is restricted, you could have a breakfast bar, or a fold-away or pull-out table.

To save storage space Choose wall-mounted items, such as tin openers, spice racks, kitchen paper and foil dispensers etc. It ensures that work surfaces are kept clear.

Need temporary working space? Pull out a drawer and put a baking sheet or large chopping board on top.

For ease of cleaning If you have tiles on the floor, have a row of tiles put *upright* between floor and bottom of units. Then dirt can't lurk, and it's easy to reach with brush or mop.

Wall extras Don't forget to hang pictures in the kitchen if you've room on the walls. They make it look more attractive and cheerful.

Cookers

As with everything else, the kind of cooker you choose will depend on your life-style, on the fuel and the space available in your kitchen – and on your pocket! It pays, though, to choose the best.

Free-standing cookers These take up less space than split-level hobs and ovens, but do have disadvantages, such as gaps at the side and back which are difficult to clean.

Split-level ovens These are usually electric, thus are cleaner, with more reliable temperature controls, but they do, in fact, take up more space. It is a great help to have the oven above waist height for lifting foods in and out of the oven. It is also very easy to see into without having to get down on the kitchen floor!

Stay-clean/self-clean ovens/oven liners Useful, though nearly all have the self-cleaning material on three 'walls' only, so that it is still necessary to clean top and bottom! Keep a large baking tray on the floor of the oven to minimise spills.

Double ovens Some are not as economical as we are led to believe. A good idea, though, if they can be used as grill and plate warmer. The lower oven, usually smaller, uses less fuel.

Hobs If gas, ensure that the pans can stand on the cooker without tipping over. Many modern gas cookers have lightweight grids which do not support the pan off the heat. Check, too, that there are no unnecessary ridges to collect dirt.

Electric hobs are easier to clean and can look more attractive, but pans must have ground bases. Ensure that there is some easily visible signal when the hob is hot.

Some split-level hobs are now available with two gas rings and two electric plates. The heat retention of the plates is useful, while the gas is more controllable for sauces etc.

Controls Make sure that the controls are no more complicated than you think you will need. Keep as simple as possible; if you are not very organised, will you make use of a timer, spit etc?

Control erosion If words or numerals on cooker or hob controls are eroding with use (you can spend an amazing 500 hours a year cooking!), paint or ink them in more clearly, and then cover with clear nail varnish.

Solid fuel cookers Some are fired by gas and oil too, and they are a way of life to many people. They take up a lot of space, but are very versatile and can be used as water heaters, clothes airers etc. The ovens do not need much cleaning. It is not so easy to regulate temperature, so cakes may be difficult to make initially (though once mastered, the results are just as good as in other cookers).

Ideal for a large, family kitchen in the country, they are not so suited to small kitchens, especially in the summer, when their warmth, welcoming in winter, can be a trial!

Ventilation In a kitchen which has no other means of ventilation, an extractor fan or cooker hood is very useful to remove steam and cooking smells. Saves on decorations too.

Oven doors Make sure they hang the right way for your kitchen. I find a drop-down door better than a side-opening door, as it gives a surface on which to rest the dishes or tins while basting or adding food.

For back sufferers If the main user of the cooker cannot bend down easily, a split-level wall-mounted oven may be the answer. A Christmas turkey, for instance, can be extremely heavy, and should be lifted with great care and *properly*, from a squatting position.

Safety in the kitchen The home is responsible for more deaths than are caused by traffic accidents, so safety in the kitchen should be a prime consideration, especially if there are children in the house. Choose a hob with its plates set back from the front, and ideally the controls should be out of reach of small hands as well.

Cookers should never be near a window or a draught: curtains could easily catch light if blown across the hob, or pilot lights could be extinguished, causing a dangerous build-up of gas.

Choose a non-slip floor surface, and mop up any spills quickly.

Fridges and freezers

Most kitchens will have a fridge as part of the work 'triangle' (see page 2), but freezers are still considered a luxury – though to me, very much a necessity. Never buy one of either that is too small – a rough size guide for a fridge is 1 cu. ft per member of the family; for a freezer, 2 cu. ft per person plus an extra 2 cu. ft. (At least this for keen gardeners who want to freeze their own produce.)

Choosing a fridge The ideal is wide and shallow so that even things at the back are easily accessible. But in a small kitchen it is best to choose a tall one that takes up less floor space.

Do you need a freezer? If only storing ready-frozen foods, then a larger fridge with a freezing compartment will be adequate. Many fridge/freezers come in one unit, for the cook who wishes to store limited home-produced food. Chest freezers are for the serious freezer cook with the space to house them. A large garage is ideal – preferably near to the kitchen.

Where to put your fridge Ideally, put it in the coldest place possible, and leave at least 1 in (2.5 cm) space between fridge and wall, so that air can circulate around the back and sides. This saves considerably on running costs (the fridge doesn't have to work so hard), but convenience usually dictates that it's in the preparation area of the kitchen, however warm it is.

Organising your fridge Store raw meat and fish in the coolest part at the top (or the section nearest the evaporator), cooked food and fats in the centre and salad ingredients at the bottom in the crisper drawer. Store eggs in the centre, and dairy products in the door.

Star markings One, two or three stars on a fridge means that it can store *already frozen food only* for up to 1 week, up to 1 month, and up to 3 months respectively. A large star to the left of 3 smaller stars distinguishes an appliance – a freezer – that can actually *freeze* food as opposed to just storing already frozen food.

Choosing a freezer Uprights take up less space in a kitchen, and their shape makes it easier to find things. They do cost more to run, as cold air escapes very rapidly whenever the door is opened. Chest freezers need more space – house in a larder, cellar or outhouse.

Don't buy a chest freezer if you have a bad back or are very tiny – you might not be able to reach the bottom!

Organising a freezer Put the heaviest and least used foods, such as the turkey for Christmas, at the bottom of a chest freezer or at the back of an upright. This saves having to lift them in and out each time you need something else out.

Storage temperatures Best temperature for short-term storage of perishable foods in a refrigerator is between 34°F and 44°F (1°C and 7°C).

Most fridges have numbers to set by – check instructions!

Defrosting the fridge Ideally defrost the fridge once a week before you do your weekly shop. Speed up the job by filling the ice tray with very hot water and put it back in the freezing compartment. Don't use detergent on the inside; bicarbonate of soda solution works best and doesn't flavour the food. Use 1 teaspoon bicarbonate to 1 pint (550 ml) hot water.

Storing food in the fridge This is a rough guide, so be sure to check use-by dates and actually *use* by that date. Wrap all foods well in clingfilm.

Butter and fats	4 weeks	Apples, citrus etc.	up to 2 weeks
Fish	1–2 days		
Leftovers	1 day	Soft fruit	2 days
Meat joints	4 days	Green veg	2 days
Salads	2 days	Root veg	2 weeks

Watch your floors! A full freezer is extraordinarily heavy – especially an upright, in which the weight is much more concentrated – so do make sure your floor can stand up to it!

Watch that swing! The swing of the fridge door can often affect the whole design of the kitchen, since it is essential that there is a setting-down space at the door-opening side.

Pots, pans and baking dishes

Once you have your kitchen planned, and you have bought your major appliances – cooker, fridge and freezer – you can have fun choosing all the basic utensils you need. Nowadays there is a wide choice of colours, finishes and materials, but you must always select the right pots and pans for your cooker, for your style of cooking.

Basic pots and pans For a well-stocked kitchen, you should have 3–4 saucepans of varying sizes and depths, with lids; 2 casseroles with lids (1 flameproof); 2 frying pans (1 with a lid); 1 omelette pan; 1 colander; 2 roasting tins of different sizes; 1 non-stick pan for milk and sauces; and 1 deep frying-pan with basket (or an electric deep-fat frier, which is safer, see page 16).

Optional extras A large saucepan of about 15 pt (8.5 L) capacity is useful for bulk cooking or preserving; a sauté pan; a griddle; gratin dishes and oval terrines; a double boiler or steamer.

What to look for Good pans should conduct heat evenly, with a diameter that is similar to the plate or burner in use. The inside should be smooth with rounded corners, and the lids should fit tightly. Handles should be in a heat-resistant material (as should the lid knobs), and should be firmly fixed and a comfortable length.

Pans to suit your cooker On my solid fuel cooker nothing but the best heavy ground-base pans will do. These are the most suitable for electricity too, and with gas you can use almost anything. I would use non-stick (Silverstone is best) for convenience if I could, as they are so useful and save so much time in cleaning (sauces, milk, scrambled eggs), but I would have to cost in a replacement set every 2 years as the coating just doesn't last.

Aluminium A good conductor of heat and cooks evenly. It is quite heavy, so suitable for electricity, but may discolour (boil tomatoes or rhubarb in lots of water in the pan to clean).

Stainless steel Durable, easy to clean and does not react to certain foods (like aluminium does), but is a poor heat conductor. It comes out of the dishwasher sparkling clean.

Cast iron Good and heavy but needs a thin coating of oil after use to prevent it rusting. Now available in non-stick from Le Creuset.

Ceramic glass and copper The former is safe at extremes of temperature, but is not a good heat conductor. I can't find a use for the latter!

Basic baking equipment For someone really interested in making cakes and breads: 2 × 7 in (17.5 cm) round sandwich tins; 1 × 7 in (17.5 cm) deep cake tin; 1 × 8 in (20 cm) cake tin, round or square; 1 × 2 lb (900 g) and 1 × 1 lb (450 g) loaf tins; a rectangular tin of 11 × 7 in (27.5 × 17.5 cm); 2 bun or patty tins (for buns and tartlets as well as Yorkshire pud); 2 pie plates; and 2 large heavy flat baking trays.

Optional extras Swiss roll tin, ring tin, brioche tin, soufflé dish, baking sheet, flans and ramekins.

Seasoning pans Frying pans particularly may stick. Brush with a small amount of oil, put 3 tablespoons salt in the pan and heat gently for about 3 minutes. With a large pad of kitchen paper rub the salt round the pan then wipe the salt away with a dry cloth. Now it won't stick!

Chip-pan dangers Chip pans which have been over-filled with fat or left unattended are frequent causes of fires. If this happens turn off the heat source. Put lid on the pan or cover with damp towel or cloth. Don't ever use water, and don't attempt to move the pan until it's cool.

Non-stick pans Clean with a non-scratch cleaner, a liquid one, and never use metal implements.

Heating milk To prevent everyday pans sticking when heating milk, first pour a little water into the bottom of the pan, heat it and *then* add milk.

Loose lids Sandwich a piece of foil between pan and lid for a closer fit.

Lid knob missing? Screw a screw through hole in lid into a cork for a temporary solution.

Bowls, dishes and plates

Dishes and plates can be the most expensive items when stocking your kitchen, so you should always choose wisely. Don't buy a patterned set unless you're sure you can live with it for years to come, and that the manufacturers will be carrying on the line to replace breakages.

How many bowls? It is vital to have several different sized bowls. Often you will be using several at once with different amounts of ingredients in each. Have at least 4 of a transparent type: 1 × 12 in (30 cm) mixing bowl; and 3 pudding basins sized ½ pt, 1 pt, and 1½ pt (300, 550 and 850 ml).

Mixing bowl Old-fashioned china mixing bowls are wider at the top than pudding basins (so you can get more air into a soufflé, egg white mix, pastry mix etc), stand firmly on their base, clean well, and can take some heat.

Non-slip bowl Put a damp cloth or sponge square under a bowl to stop it slipping around.

Wooden salad bowls A large one is wonderful for a tossed salad, and you can also find individual ones (cheaper abroad than here). They need special care to prevent the wood losing its colour and drying out. Never wash in the dishwasher, and occasionally feed the wood after washing with a few drops of salad oil.

Choosing bowls I like to have a selection of various kinds of bowls, but glass is very useful. They can be used for normal mixing and whipping, but can also double as serving bowls.

Capacity reminder Write the capacity of the bowl on the under-side with a waterproof marker pen; this helps when making a mousse or soufflé. (You can also mark or scratch on the bottom of baking dishes.)

Whipping problems If your working surface is the wrong height for comfortable lengthy whipping, put the bowl on top of a cloth in the sink, and whip to your arm's content!

Choosing plates I would never select too busy a pattern, as I think it conflicts with the presentation of the food. Let your *food* be the picture. A simple design on a basic white is the most effective, and you can play around more with colours of tablecloths, napkins, place mats etc to ring the changes on your dinner table.

Serving dishes Those in which you can both cook and serve are good, and because they have a double function, take up much less space in the kitchen. Avoid those fancy vegetable dishes without flat bases as they don't keep the food hot.

Special occasion serving Although I'm all for keeping china and plates to a minimum, I like to have a few 'specials'. Shell china dishes (or actual half scallop shells) are wonderful for starters, and I have some dearly loved half-moon plates for side salads. Many other 'specials' exist, such as artichoke, avocado, escargot, oyster, and corn-on-the-cob dishes.

Serving glasses Never forget that your prettier drinking glasses can make very effective serving dishes for colourful desserts like trifles.

Cocottes and ramekins Often available as seconds or in sales, these are invaluable for starters, tiny vegetable baking dishes, and for puddings. They are oven-proof and many are also freezer-proof. They make good presents, too, so either give them or ask for them!

Improvising ramekins If your birthday hasn't come round yet, and you *haven't* got enough ramekins to make, say, small mousses for a dinner party – improvise with foil. Shape double foil around the outside of one of your few remaining ramekins, folding so that it fits tightly, and the inside is smooth. Then proceed as normal.

Looking after earthenware Soak unglazed earthenware cooking dishes in cold water for about 20 minutes before using to prevent cracking. Don't ever wash with liquid detergent as they're very porous; simply soak in hot water with some salt added.

Protecting fine plates Store carefully with a piece of soft kitchen paper between each plate. Never pile too high or the pressure on the bottom plate may crack it.

Cutlery and knives

The choice of style, material and price of cutlery is, of course, a matter for individual taste, but durability, pleasure and comfort, and ease of cleaning, are major considerations. Kitchen knives are another vital ingredient in the well-stocked kitchen, and they should really be of the finest quality.

Stainless steel cutlery This is the cheapest cutlery, although it may rise in price according to manufacturer, finish, design etc. This is the best choice if you use a dishwasher.

Non-metal handles Cutlery can have wood, bone, ivory, china or stoneware handles. These, of course, should not be put in the dishwasher, and indeed many won't stand prolonged immersion in water. Wash the prongs and blades only if you can; the fixative on many knife handles, for instance, is a resin which expands when wet or hot, and the handle could thus come away from the blade.

For easy washing-up For any cutlery, but particularly that with non-metal handles, have a jug of hot soapy water at the side of the sink, and put used cutlery in, prongs or blades down, handles out of the water, for easy – and safer – cleaning.

Choosing cutlery Go to a large kitchen shop or department store, and *try* the cutlery out for size and comfort (just as you would before buying a bed, for instance!). Make sure the balance feels right, and that the handle sits comfortably in your palm.

Buy for your life-style Bright primary coloured handles on cutlery may look marvellous in your sunny kitchen, but will not look so good on a formal dining table.

Tablespoons Buy some proper full-sized tablespoons for measuring and serving (modern ones are very often shallow). Silver-plated spoons are cheap in junk or antique shops.

The answer to silver cleaning Everyone has one, but you will never need mammoth cleaning sessions, if every time you use your silverware, you wash it, rub with an impregnated cleaning cloth, then cover it all individually with clingfilm and store in the dark. Even my silver trays are wrapped in clingfilm . . .

Be practical For cleanliness, practicality, and sheer convenience, never have out more cutlery than you need every day. If the children are coming home for the holidays, or you have guests coming to stay, *then* bring out the extra knives, forks, spoons etc. It is also a good idea to keep utensil drawers free from unused or defunct gadgets; there's nothing more frustrating than tools which don't work!

Kitchen knives Basically they should be comfortable to hold, easy to use, designed for their particular job, and, above all, *sharp*. I would suggest the following as essential: carving set of knife, fork and sharpening steel (in the absence of the latter, a wall-mounted knife sharpener, or the back doorstep will do); a serrated bread knife, French cook's knives, a small veg knife, small palette knife, a filleting or boning knife, and a grapefruit knife (*nothing* else can do the job so efficiently).

Storage of kitchen knives Keep them separate from cutlery, and preferably not in a drawer, where blades may cut searching fingers. Wall-mount them on a magnetic rack; this way you can see at a glance which is which. Wooden blocks with knife points hidden in them, although very safe, make it a matter of trial and error which knife is pulled out.

Other cutting implements A good pair of kitchen scissors is almost as basic as knives and forks. They should be strong enough to do the toughest jobs – like cutting chicken legs off a carcass – and pointed enough to do more precise work. A good potato peeler is vital, and a wall-mounted can-opener is ten times more efficient and time-saving than butterfly hand openers.

Easy herb chopping Put your herbs in a mug and snip away at them with your kitchen scissors – much more effective than chopping on a board.

Smelly knives It sounds – and looks – crazy, but if kitchen knives persistently smell of fish or onion, plunge them into earth (garden or window box) several times (wash afterwards, of course).

Blenders, processors and mixers

These all tend to come into the more expensive areas of kitchen equipment, but are all great time-savers for the busy cook. Two or three specialist machines might be better than a large one which is never fully used. Do check specialist magazines for those which are deemed best, and shop around before buying as prices can vary astonishingly!

Time-saving Although a large initial investment, some sort of electrical mixer or blender is a great boon for every cook. They purée and shred in seconds, take the hard work out of many mixtures, and can do many things that are difficult – if not impossible – by hand.

Hand mixers These are inexpensive, can be wall-mounted, and are useful for dishes which need whisking while cooking (zabaglione, for example). They are also handy for whipping up cream and meringue, which need *your* control (a large machine could *over*-whip). Most small mixers only have a small motor, though, which can be overworked.

Mixers If you do a lot of cooking, especially baking, these are invaluable. Choose one with a variety of speeds, as those with only a single high-speed motor are unsuitable for many mixtures – mayonnaise, for instance. Many have a lot of attachments, but make sure you want them *before* you buy; buy only the basics at first, then add the extras as and when you feel you need them.

Liquidisers These can be the greatest time-saver of all – vital for puréeing vegetables, making soups, and preparing baby food (make in 'bulk' and freeze in small batches – in ice-cube trays). Look for a good substantial capacity for family use, though; many are very small.

Processors More useful than a liquidiser as capacity is usually larger, and engine more powerful. It must be capable of chopping meat for beefburgers, and liver etc into different textures for pâté (although it can *over*-process if you're not careful). Useful for making mayonnaise and soups, also all-in-one cakes.

Mincers These are obviously useful for preparing meat for pâtés, beefburgers etc. They can be difficult to clean, and they do tend to rust easily if not thoroughly dried. After dismantling, keep the screws in a bag to prevent them getting lost. My mincer has now been replaced by a processor.

Cleaning a mincer After mincing meat, cheese or anything sticky, mince some stale bread through the machine. The crumbs are not suitable for domestic use – but the birds will enjoy them!

Keep them handy A processor, mixer or liquidiser, to be truly useful, must be kept within easy reach, preferably on the working surface near its electric point. Keep the most used attachments nearby, and any others together in a nearby cupboard or drawer.

Cleaning a blender goblet or processor Half fill with warm, slightly soapy water and switch on for a few moments. This will whisk away any stuck food particles.

Variety is the spice of life Don't just use your liquidiser or blender for the most obvious things. Many have a multitude of less likely uses. Whisk granulated sugar into castor in a few seconds if you've run out; lentils or rice can be ground into a flour to add to soups or stews to thicken nutritiously and tastily; chop dried fruit, nuts, chocolate, bread for crumbs. It will even shred ice (useful for those icy drinks that children seem to love; add squash or fresh fruit juice). Make instant garlic butter, or a sandwich spread with butter, a little stock, cheese or leftovers.

Hand graters Not a machine, of course, but vital in the kitchen for grating, from lemon peel to nutmeg. To sharpen blunt graters, rub them with coarse sandpaper, and wash well before using again. To clean them after use, make sure you've wasted none of that peel by brushing the inside with a pastry brush, then wash with a stiff nylon brush in hot soapy water.

Other cooking equipment

These are some of the many other cooking appliances which are used in general for more specialised or economical cooking. None are vital, but can save time, money, or are just simply fun!

Barbecues These range from the simplest biscuit tin with holes and a grid, to a permanent brick structure, or a sophisticated gas machine on wheels. Some friends even had the ultimate in moveable barbecues in a metal wheelbarrow! Barbecued food is always delicious and turns the simplest beefburger into a feast.

Cleaning barbecues Line the base and sides with foil to minimise cleaning – the shiny side up also intensifies the heat. Clean racks immediately by soaking in a sink of hot soapy (Ariel) water.

To speed up barbecue time Pre-cook food like chicken pieces for half the cooking time in a microwave or conventional oven. This helps the food cook inside before the outside is browned.

Deep-fat friers These are a good idea, replacing the chip pan with an extremely safe, odour-free gadget. Healthier than shallow frying as the correct temperature seals the food immediately and prevents it absorbing excess grease. Change the filter frequently to preserve the quality of the oil – change the oil occasionally too!

Fondue This is a fun way to cook food, and to turn a meal into a special occasion. Buy a metal one for meat and ceramic for cheese, unless you can afford a Le Creuset or similar, which is perfect for both. The number of guests that can be accommodated at one time is limited, and for a meat fondue, top-quality steak is a must!

Fondue forks Always buy twice the number of special fondue forks. A meat fondue can be a lengthy and hungry business if only one forkful is cooking at a time. Make sure forks are differentiated in some way – different colours perhaps – so that thieving is kept to a minimum! Steel meat skewers may be used as a last resort but remember to supply suitable cloths or napkins with which to remove them from the bowl when hot.

Microwave ovens The main advantage is speed. It is possible to take a dish from the freezer, defrost it (sometimes that's not even necessary), and cook it in a very short time. They perform best when cooking small quantities, and some models now have browning elements and convection cooking. They are economical, although require special dishes.

Handy microwave hints Small sprigs of leaves or herbs can be dried in the microwave; tomatoes and peaches can be skinned easily; dried fruit can be plumped up in water; and nuts or breadcrumbs can be toasted in seconds.

Multi-cookers Sometimes called electric frying or cook pans, they can roast, steam, poach, braise, stew, fry, sauté – as well as make yogurt and popcorn! Although they take up a lot of working-surface space, they can cook a chicken in half the time of an ordinary oven.

Pressure cookers These are economical, but don't cook things like green veg well. Good for suet puddings, beetroot, tough cuts of meats, stews – anything in fact, if suitable, that would take over 2 hours to cook.

Wok Works well with gas, but takes rather longer to heat up on electricity, thereby defeating the intended principle of quick frying. It makes meat go a long way, and is very healthy (very little fat is needed). It can also work as a steamer.

Caring for your wok Oil lightly after drying, then cover with clingfilm so that the oil doesn't get covered in unappetising dust.

Sandwich maker A boon for households with children. If the seal is tight enough (vital) the most liquid of fillings can be enclosed in a sandwich. Butter the bread on the outside for a good finish.

Slow cooker These are useful for well-organised people, as the food can be prepared the night before, or in the morning before going to work, then switched on and left throughout the day. It is ideal for cooking meat, as the low temperature stops the meat from shrinking, and it makes wonderfully clear stock. Economical to use, and a great help at a busy time like Christmas as an extra independently controlled pan. If making chilli con carne, boil the red kidney beans for a good 10 minutes first. They are poisonous if not boiled properly.

Other kitchen necessities

Everyone has different necessities, depending on their style of cooking, and I couldn't possibly mention everything. The following are just a few of those without which I couldn't survive!

Sieves These are essential if you don't have a liquidiser or vegetable mill, and can also be used for flour and sugar sifting, and straining. The largest are the most useful. Use stainless steel for vegetable purées or soup making, and hair or nylon for seedless fruit mousses, etc.

Scales Balance scales with weights are ideal if you haven't a space problem – they need to be handy on the work surface. But wall-mounted are useful as they're out of the way, and you don't have to bend. Any scale, though, must be able to weigh *small* as well as *large*.

Lost small weights? Improvise with coins. A 2p piece or 2 × 1 p pieces weigh ¼ oz, 1½ p weighs 5 g, and 3 p weighs approximately 10 g.

Skewers Get *straight* ones – twisted ones are difficult to clean – and hang on nails or string in the larder in varying sizes. Use for kebabs, obviously, but they're also good if very fine for testing if a cake is ready, and for spearing potatoes before baking (they cook the potatoes more quickly as the heat is conducted right into the centre).

Spatulas Plastic, very flexible spatulas are good for scraping every last drop of a mixture out of a bowl, and for scraping the debris off a working surface after rolling pastry.

Piping bags Improvise if stuck by cutting the corner off the bottom of a paper or plastic bag. If you have a proper bag, clean it out thoroughly by holding under a hot tap, followed by a final wash in the washing machine.

Thermometer Useful if you're doubtful about the efficiency of your oven. To test if the thermometer itself is accurate, put it in hot water in a pan and bring gradually to the boil, checking it registers boiling point – 212°F, 100°C.

Foil The kitchen necessity, I believe, and I use 2 widths, wall-mounted in dispensers. It excludes light and air, is non-absorbent, non-perishable, and doesn't let smell or flavour out *or* in. I use it to wrap for the freezer (then in a poly bag), to line cake tins and the barbecue, to substitute as a lid for casseroles, to cover baking sheets or cake bases if a bit tatty, and as a baking 'dish' (a foil-wrapped fish or potato, or a chop or chicken breast with a little seasoning, butter and wine), so all the goodness and juices are kept firmly in the food.

Further foil virtues I also line enamel plates with foil for a non-stick pastry pie dish; cover a Christmas pudding with doubled and pleated foil; and make little extra containers with foil. A doubled long strip of foil can be put under a steamed pudding in the pan; this is then easy to lift out by the two ends. For tray-baked cakes, mould foil round the *outside* of a roasting tin then put *inside* the tin so that the side meeting the cake is smooth. If baking in a loose-bottomed flan tin, cover the outside with foil to prevent any spillage.

Clingfilm This too is extraordinarily useful for keeping foods fresh in the fridge – and you can see what's in the packet without opening it. Wrap cheese, the cut half of a butter pack, slices of lemon for gin and tonic, etc. Is useful for sandwiches, as wrapping for packed lunches and picnics, and is invaluable for covering foods for a buffet party if there's no room in the fridge.

Kitchen roll Essential for kitchen sneezes and tears (hopefully not many of either), but I use it to soak fat off the top of casseroles, for mopping up generally, for draining veg after blanching, and for polishing my black glass oven door and the kitchen windows. It's also soft enough to use for germinating mustard and cress, and even runner beans in a glass jar!

J-cloths These can also be used instead of muslin or a filter, and can be sterilised and washed in the washing machine. A small square of J-cloth is useful as the top of a jar in which you are sprouting beans or seeds. Fix with an elastic band, and then water can go in and be drained out daily without removing the lid.

The store cupboard

Make sure that your store cupboard or larder contains the sorts of food that you are likely to need and use, and not necessarily what you think you ought to have! Obviously, it will store the things you need constantly – flour, sugar, pasta, coffee, tea etc – but a few less used items can come in handy in an emergency.

Planning the store cupboard I have narrow shelves close together, just large enough to take a double row of cans, better than deep shelves where you have to stack the foods and so have to search behind things to find exactly what you want.

Organising the store cupboard Group the foods into various categories such as meat, fish, vegetables and fruit, into cans and packets, flours and sugars together, bottles and taller items to the back, and store them together so that they are easy to find. Put the least used provisions on high shelves and the items you use often within easy reach.

Rotation is the rule Although you can't tell how long the shop had the can, packet or whatever before you bought it, *you* can date-stamp everything with a waterproof marker and use it in rotation, using up old stock first, storing new items *behind* older ones.

Buying canned foods Never buy bulging cans – the food has gone off – or those with dents near the seams – air could have entered the can.

Storing canned foods They last a long time, but should be kept in a cool dry place. Milk products, prunes and rhubarb last 1 year; soft fruits and new potatoes, 18 months; other veg and fruit, baked beans, pastas, soups, fish in sauces, and ready meals, 2 years; fish in oil for 5 years.

Opened canned foods Always wipe the tin before opening, then decant – literally – for there is a slight risk that the lining of the tin can deteriorate thus spoiling the food. Be particularly meticulous if using canned baby foods.

Herbs Renew jars of dried herbs once a year. Soft leafy ones –

parsley, chervil, tarragon and chives – are best fresh from the herb garden. Or you can freeze them.

Spices Best stored away from light. Spices, particularly ground, tend to fade in flavour and colour. Whole spices are much more economical and keep for several years. Ground spices are best used within 18 months. Store vanilla pods in a jar of sugar for an (almost) instant supply of vanilla sugar.

Flour Store in the bags that it comes in rather than in a jar, and then you won't muddle the plain with the self-raising – but a small jar can stand beside the cooker for instant access for sauces etc. Flour, porridge oats and semolina should all be used within 4 months once opened.

Oil and vinegar Keep in their separate bottles, obviously, but why not make a store-cupboard French dressing in a 3 pt (1.7 L) quantity. Keep one-third out for use, and store remainder in fridge.

Dried fruits Be sure that these are wrapped well so they don't dry out. Once the pack is opened, slip the remainder into a polythene bag and seal. If you've over-bought, store the remainder in the freezer, well wrapped, and use within 2 years.

Nuts (and chocolate) If after Christmas you find you have masses of nuts left over, store them in the freezer (they won't go rancid). Store each variety of shelled nut in a labelled poly bag and then put them all together in a large bag. Whole nuts should be stored separately, and used within a year. Shelled will keep for up to 2 years. (Chocolate keeps better in the freezer too.)

Store-cupboard emergencies Many canned foods can literally save the day. Use tuna in salads or bakes; anchovies on pizzas; salmon in sandwiches; sardines for quick pâté or dip; corned beef for salad or hash; condensed soups for sauces (mushrooms, tomato and crab bisque are particularly useful); consommé in mousses; pimentoes for decoration; sweetcorn for chowders; tomatoes for *everything*; various beans in salads; celery with a white or cheese sauce; and baby onions to add to casseroles.

Shopping

To some this is a chore, to some a pleasure – but whichever it is to you, it's always best, both economically and time-wise, to be well organised, to buy seasonally and sensibly.

Checklist Keep a permanent checklist of basic items inside your store-cupboard door, then you can quickly run your eye down it before going out shopping. List there items in terms of Flavourings and Seasonings – herbs, salt, mustard etc – Staples such as rice, flour or sugar, and Canned Foods.

Memo board When you run out of something from your store cupboard, have a memo board for jotting it down on, then you won't forget what it is when you go out shopping. Encourage other members of the family to do so too.

Planning the menu Try to plan for at least a few days ahead before you shop, choosing seasonal combinations of meat or fish plus fruit and vegetables.

Shopping lists Make a shopping list based on your checklist, memo board and menu plan, and group together the things *sold* together, to save doubling back in the supermarket or going to other shops.

Save money Take your own light folding shopping bag inside your handbag rather than pay for plastic bags in the supermarket.

Supermarket bargain bins Good idea if you can see the quality and you can use the same day, say fresh vegetables, ripe fruit etc. Only be tempted by special offers if you are *sure* they will benefit you.

Sell-by dates Always check these on tins, packets and packages before buying. Be sure you are going to be able to use before the date expires.

For health Start checking, too, the listed contents of cans, jars, etc. Many have horrifying lists of artificial and fattening ingredients. Buy only the purest, and teach children to look at labels too.

Frozen food If you know you are going to buy a quantity of frozen food, go armed with newspaper to wrap it in, or even better take an insulated picnic bag or box. Get it home quickly.

Filling shopping trolley or basket Put heavy firm things at the bottom – cans, root veg etc – and then lighter packets or squashy things on top.

Bulk buying This saves making several journeys and saves shopping time. Buy things you use a lot of – but not perishable things – in bulk if you have room to store them: washing powder, fruit squashes, toilet paper, canned fruit, cat food, washing-up liquid etc.

Home delivery Take advantage of the milkman's offer to deliver things such as potatoes, lemonade and fruit juices if you haven't your own transport. It saves lugging heavy shopping home yourself.

Watch your back If you have to lift heavy boxes, do so from a squatting position, *not* by leaning over from the hips. Carrier bags, one on either side to balance you, are often better. Shopping trolleys can sometimes strain shoulder and back.

Quantities of food to buy for average portions

Fish

Crabs	1 small
Cutlets	8 oz (225 g)
Fillets	6–8 oz (175–225 g)
Fish, whole	½–¾ lb (225–350 g)
Lobster	½–¾ lb (225–350 g)
Mussels	1 pt (550 ml)
Prawns	½ pint (300 ml)

Fruit for cooking	4–8 oz (110–225 g)

Meat

cooked	2–3 oz (50–75 g)
with bone	½–¾ lb (225–350 g)
without bone	4–6 oz (110–175 g)

Vegetables

Asparagus	6-8 stalks
Celery	½ head
Mushrooms, dried beans, peas	2–4 oz (50–110 g)
Tomatoes	4–6 oz (110–175 g)
Green beans, beetroot, sprouts, cabbage, carrots, swedes	6–8 oz (175–225 g)
Leeks, marrow, parsnips, fresh peas, potatoes, spinach	8 oz (225 g)

Cutting corners in the kitchen

Everyone wants to save money, and 'waste not want not' should be the phrase on the lips of all who run an efficient kitchen. Cutting corners also means improvising and substituting, and often the results are no different!

Save fuel Make sure that saucepans cover the electric plate or that gas flames don't lick up sides of pan, otherwise you are wasting energy. And if cooker-top space is at a premium, use a simple bain marie. Fill a roasting tin with water; this can sit on one burner with 3 or 4 small pans or bowls inside it.

Two at a time Use one pan for cooking two different vegetables at the same time by putting each vegetable in a boil-in-the-bag polythene bag.

Leftover wine, beer or cider Decant any that is left in a bottle or can into a small bottle: keep in the refrigerator for up to 3 weeks, or put in a container in the freezer for up to 2 months.

Drawer liners Use leftover wallpaper to line drawers and cupboards.

Foil containers Save foil containers from convenience or take-away foods: they are a handy size for cooking small portions in, or storing in the freezer.

The last of a sponge or madeira cake While still fresh, freeze together with any leftover marzipan, icing or cake trimmings. Use to make truffles, trifle or something similar at a later date.

Half a cream cake left after Sunday tea? Cut into wedges, wrap each individually, and freeze. Take out a couple of wedges when someone drops in unexpectedly (they will thaw in 30 minutes).

Not enough cake tins? Make foil ones. Place a double thickness of foil over the outside of a soufflé or oven-glass dish and press down the sides. Trim off any surplus, brush with melted fat, and stand on baking sheet to give extra support.

No large mixing bowl? If you're making a huge Christmas

pudding, or preparing for a party, use a baby's bath, a scrubbed washing-up bowl, or even a clean bucket!

Quick funnel Cut the corner off a large brown envelope and use it as a funnel for dry items such as flour or sugar.

Toffee trays These can often be bought very cheaply from sweet shops. They are easy to stack and store – use for toffee, shortbread, or as open-freezing trays.

For quickly chopped walnuts Put them in a poly bag and crush them with a rolling pin (it's the best way to crush biscuits or cornflakes too).

To clarify dripping Simply put it in a pan with some water, bring to the boil slowly, allowing the fat to melt. Chill and the clean fat will be hardened on the top, and any debris will be at the bottom. Store in the fridge, and use in non-meat recipes.

Vanilla sugar Put a couple of vanilla pods in a jar of caster sugar, cover with a lid, and leave. Stir from time to time. Much cheaper and better than deli vanilla sugar, and you just top it up with more sugar when necessary.

Lemon sugar (or tea) Just add thinly peeled dried orange or lemon zest to caster sugar and store as above. (Add it to loose tea, and you'll have a wonderfully flavoured – and cheap – cuppa.)

Bacon pieces Buy these to use in a quiche instead of cutting up whole rashers. They're cheaper, but can be a bit salty so go easy on that when using them.

Smoked salmon pieces Watch out for these at the deli. Ideal for making a pâté; process 8 oz (225 g) smoked salmon with the same amount of butter, 4 oz (110 g) rich cream cheese, juice of ½ lemon and black pepper. Pack in a small dish and eat with toast.

Compost For those in the country or with a large garden, keep a separate bucket for the compost heap – veg peelings, outside leaves, egg shells, tea leaves, coffee grounds etc. Wastage doesn't seem so awful if you're making use of it!

Following a recipe

This may seem simplistic, but many failures occur because quantities have been measured wrongly, the method has been misinterpreted, or the heat has been too high or low. Even the best cook, when preparing a dish for the first time, needs to follow the instructions to the letter!

Choosing a recipe Choose seasonally and for the occasion, and choose something that you and your family are likely to enjoy eating. Don't embark on a recipe just because the idea appeals to you.

Get to know the recipe first Read it through and make sure that you have all the ingredients and equipment to hand that it asks for. Experienced and confident cooks *can* substitute or improvise, but it's better to do it exactly the first time.

The first stage Collect together all the ingredients and equipment. If the method is short and you are using the oven, switch it to the correct temperature to heat up before you start cooking.

Get to know your oven Many recipes are spoiled by wayward ovens – each heats differently, and some aren't accurate. Get to know yours, and check with an oven thermometer if you're distrustful.

Oven temperatures Some recipes call for a 'cool' or 'moderate' oven. Here are the facts!

Very cool	225°F	110°C	Gas ¼
	250°F	120°C	Gas ½
Cool	275°F	140°C	Gas 1
	300°F	150°C	Gas 2
Moderate	325°F	160°C	Gas 3
	350°F	180°C	Gas 4
Moderately hot	375°F	190°C	Gas 5
	400°F	200°C	Gas 6
Hot	425°F	220°C	Gas 7
	450°F	230°C	Gas 8
Very hot	475°F	240°C	Gas 9

Following a recipe for the first time Prepare and work meticulously and tick off the ingredients as you use them in order to ensure that nothing is missed out!

Adapting a recipe After preparing and trying out the finished dish, you may well want to alter it. Note down any alterations you have made or would like to make, and then you will remember next time. Also, if you find it serves more people than the recipe suggests then jot this down too. All these notes will add to future success.

Keeping the recipe book clean Pop it inside a clean polythene bag, make a jacket cover with clingfilm, or just cover the open pages with clingfilm and fix with sticky tape.

On measuring ingredients A novice cook should always measure ingredients accurately until the 'feel' of cooking is attained. More experienced cooks know that measuring down to the last grain of salt is not always necessary. A little less stock or a little more onion will probably not make all that much difference.

Use your judgement In recipes that call for Cheddar cheese, say, you will have to make up your own mind about measurements and final taste. Cheddar varies from the mildest to the strongest, and you may need to use less or more for taste success.

Salt to taste When a recipe says this or 'season to taste', it means precisely that. It's up to *you*. But remember that salt can never be *subtracted*, and if a sauce or stock has to be simmered for a long time, the salt taste will intensify.

'Vague' measurements These can be confusing. A pinch is what you can pick up between forefinger and thumb – or ⅛ teaspoon or less. A knob of butter is walnut sized, about ½ oz (15 g).

Handy small measurements For flour for soups, sauces etc, use a tablespoon. *Rounded* is 1 oz (25 g), *level* (flatten with a knife blade) is ½ oz (15 g).

Measuring liquids Put the measuring jug on the work surface, wait until the liquid stops moving, then bend down to check the level accurately.

Metric versus Imperial Use one or the other, and never upset the proportions by switching over during the preparation of the recipe.

Understanding terms and techniques If there's an instruction you don't understand, refer to a good cookery book's glossary – which should explain all!

Menu planning

Whether planning for a special occasion or for the week's family eating, a good meal has to have the right balance. You have to think of rich versus bland, contrasts of colour, flavour and texture, the right combination of vitamins, protein, etc.

General guidelines for healthy eating Most of this is common knowledge and sense. Fresh is best. Eat plenty of raw or lightly cooked vegetables, and raw fruit. Avoid manufactured, refined or processed foods as much as possible. Cut out sugar and saturated fat (in butter and some meats) as far as you can, and eat foods rich in fibre (formerly known as roughage).

Healthy cooking methods Try to avoid frying food, especially in additional fat (use a non-stick pan which doesn't need extra grease); cook meat or poultry with a little vegetable oil or in its own fat; braise, steam or grill in preference to roasting or frying; use minimum of water and cooking time for vegetables (and always use the stock for soups or sauces).

Think of alternative proteins Meat and fish are major protein sources, but also contain fat which is bad for your health if eaten in excess. Try to get into the habit of serving a few 'vegetarian' or meatless meals during the week – macaroni cheese, for instance (wholemeal pasta for carbohydrate, and cheese for protein), or a lentil dish (all pulses contain a lot of protein).

Vary meals sensibly Balance the *daily* intake of your family by varying elements and foods – serve eggs for breakfast, cheese for lunch, and meat for supper, for instance. A good breakfast is essential, with fresh fruit or juice and some protein to get everyone going. Lunch can be light and dinner more substantial (or vice versa), but there is truth in the old saying: 'Breakfast like a king, lunch like a prince and dine like a pauper'!

Get the calories right Make sure that each meal as a whole is not too filling or fattening, by balancing heavier ingredients or courses with lighter ones.

Planning a dinner party It is often easiest to choose the main course first, then a complementary starter and dessert can be selected.

Get the meal balance right If serving a simple roast with a thin gravy, you could have a richer starter – a creamy soup, perhaps. If serving an exotic spicy casserole, a vegetable starter like artichoke or avocado would be appropriate.

Get the colours right Don't serve a chicken blanquette with rice for main course after a pale soup and followed by a cream dessert. The colours are boring, and one of the major joys of eating is the pleasure given *visually* by the food. It's easy to vary the colours and look of food, even if only by colourful garnishes.

Get the textures right Accompany a smooth soup with crunchy croûtons, tiny bits of a related vegetable, or garlic bread, wholemeal toast or Melba toast. Cook vegetables so that they still have bite, add chopped nuts to vegetable purées. Chewing is good for us, so never make the mistake of serving say, mashed potatoes, purées and things like soufflés or mousses in the same meal.

Menu planning for economy For meals in winter especially, you can save on fuel by planning to make full use of oven space – everything from starter to pudding (or as much as is feasible) could be cooked in the oven.

Lacking time or money? If entertaining, or even if just feeding the family, never be afraid to serve the simplest food. As long as it is cooked properly, and is of the best quality, it will be appreciated. A salad can be served as a starter instead of accompanying the main course, and a couple of good cheeses or a bowl of fresh fruit can be the perfect end to a meal.

Forward planning Many would scoff, but as many people work to an actual weekly or monthly meal plan, some sort of organisation like this is invaluable for the busy family cook. Even if you don't want to introduce the 'If it's mince it must be Monday syndrome, you could designate Monday a cold meat day (with a baked potato), Thursday the non-meat day, and Friday for fish.

Easy entertaining

For a trouble-free party, plan your shopping and menu very carefully (pages 22–3 and 28–9 should help). A 3-course meal is quite acceptable even for comparatively formal dinner parties at home, and you should keep the recipes simple.

Choosing recipes Select those that need the minimum of last-minute preparations (guests have come to see and talk to *you*, and you shouldn't need to be in the kitchen all the time). And also choose dishes that will not spoil if kept waiting, either by late guests, or by that absorbing conversation over drinks.

Getting the timing right Work out an approximate timetable. Estimate how long it will take to prepare each dish, then you can work out in which order to do things so that the meal is ready at the right time. Allow at least 15 minutes spare for all the emergencies – phone calls, callers and other crises – that always crop up during the day, and allow your guests time to be late and to have a relaxed drink before they eat.

Hot or cold? This depends on oven space, principally, and to a certain extent on the season, but 1 hot course could be flanked by 2 cold courses, or if you want a hot starter as well as hot main courses, choose one that can be prepared on top of the cooker.

Advance preparation To avoid stress on the day, many dishes can be prepared well in advance – home-made soups and many puddings, for example. Many casseroles can be made the day before (or even taken out of the freezer), and reheated with only accompanying vegetables or garnishes to be prepared from scratch.

The starter Keep it simple, and don't hesitate to buy something ready-made if you're busy – like smoked mackerel, potted shrimps or pâté. Serve with an interesting garnish and freshly made toast. (Most meat and fish pâtés taste better if left for 2 hours at room temperature before serving. Wrap in clingfilm to retain moisture.)

Main courses Pre-cooked braises or stews are by far the easiest, and they can range from the simplest beef stew to a goulash or casserole of game. Try to avoid last-minute dishing-up by using oven-to-table ware. Make sure you have heat-resistant mats to protect the table.

Reheating Allow 20–30 minutes longer for a dish from the fridge than for one at room temperature. The time involved will also depend on the size of the dish. Deep dishes take longer to reheat than shallow ones, and so do ovenglass dishes compared to metal ones.

Covering dishes and casseroles Cover with a lid or piece of foil when keeping hot to prevent drying out. The best temperature at which to keep food hot is about 250°F/120°C/Gas ½. Don't keep foods hot for too long, as some lose flavour and colour.

Last-minute attention When serving a dish that needs some of this, be sure to have everything ready right down to the hot serving dish, the chopped parsley, and garnish, and then it will just need assembling.

Forgotten to heat the plates? Simply plunge them into hot water in the sink and leave for a few minutes.

Vegetables These should usually be served the minute they are cooked, and if you have everything else organised, no one will resent a few minutes' absence while you steam, boil al dente or stir-fry. But many veg can be baked or braised as well – red cabbage, tomatoes, celery, potatoes, fennel etc.

Desserts Sorbets and icecreams *need* to be made in advance (but remember to allow them time in the fridge before serving to become the right texture); and meringue or Pavlova can have been baked ahead, stored in an airtight tin, then filled with whipped cream and fruit 2 hours before serving.

Cheese Stand for at least an hour out of the fridge before serving to allow flavour to develop. I usually serve only 2 cheeses, one unusual and a good Cheddar, for instance. Serve on vine or blackcurrant leaves, with grapes.

Slimming wisdom

Whether you are catering for a slimmer in the family or you are dieting yourself, much slimming wisdom is the same as healthy eating (see Menu Planning). Slim is healthy, but don't ever become obsessed: many people just are bigger than others!

The basics Avoid frying above all, and fill up with vegetables – raw, lightly steamed or boiled – and fresh fruit. Both are a valuable source of vitamins and fibre (although beware of bananas and avocados which are high in calories).

Diet sensibly Don't go on a diet of less than 1000 calories per day without taking prior medical advice.

Take it seriously Try to approach the diet in the right frame of mind – that is, you are going to stick to it, you are going to like it – and this will help enormously.

Don't get bored Avoid monotony, otherwise you will soon get bored. Vary colours and textures.

Fill the plate Either make your plate look full up with salad, or serve your meals on smaller plates!

Don't cheat The odd biscuit here and there can undo all the good of several days' careful eating. Don't ever try to eat up what the children have left – throw it away!

Eating between meals Avoid this if you can. If hungry have a cup of hot Bovril or munch low-calorie celery, cucumber or carrot sticks, or cauliflower sprigs. Fruit and vegetables are a good choice 'to fill that hole'. Being a good source of roughage, they quite soon satisfy hunger-pangs.

Count your calories Get yourself a small book on the calorie content of food. *Slimming* magazine have produced a good one.

Give yourself some kind of goal Either a special dress (a size smaller, perhaps?) or a present, once you have lost the target amount of weight. Let your family join in, they can help a lot.

Family (diet) planning Try and plan your diet to fit in with the family. They will enjoy many of the slimmer's recipes, and you can give them larger helpings. It makes hard work of a diet if you have to cook completely different meals for the family.

Thickening sauces, stews etc Instead of doing this at the beginning of cooking (meat coated in flour, for instance), do it at the end. Remove slimmer's portion, and then thicken with flour and water or beurre manié (flour and butter).

Eating out Don't be too fanatical about the calories you eat. If you do go out and eat a little more than you should out of politeness, just cut down on your next meal.

Breakfast Do eat a little breakfast otherwise you may feel rather hungry in the middle of the morning and succumb to a biscuit. A good start is half a grapefruit without sugar, a small slice of wholemeal toast with no butter, and a cup of coffee, black preferably.

Fish White fish is excellent for the dieter, and it's best poached or grilled. Oily fish should be eaten in small quantities only, grilled without fat.

Meats Eat lean meats – like chicken and turkey, but without the skin – and trim all fat off other meat. If grilling or roasting, cook on a rack and let the fat cooked out drip away.

Dairy products The lowest calorie cheeses are cottage and curd as they contain little fat (all hard cheeses are much more calorie laden). Try to use low-fat or skimmed milk. Butter, I'm afraid, is banned, but some diet margarines are good.

Fats Use a minimum for cooking, and use your good non-stick pans which reduce the need for fat.

Bread Bread itself is not particularly full of calories, but it's one of the easiest foods to load with fats such as butter, margarine or cheese – all high-calorie foods. Choose crispbreads.

Anything else? Avoid salt and cakes, biscuits and heavy puddings with cream *at all costs*!

Drinks time and simple eats

Having a drink with friends is one of the most pleasant of social occasions, and if it's allied to food – a few dips and snacks, a buffet supper or a formal dinner – it can be even more enjoyable.

What kind of party? Choose your drinks according to the type of party, and the number expected. A choice of wine or spirits or cocktails is best for a small number only, and for a large party I find it best to offer a chilled sparkling wine or Buck's Fizz (champagne or sparkling wine and fresh orange juice). Pimms is more economical than it may sound – and lovely in summer.

Glasses Make sure you have enough to cope with the expected numbers. Many wine suppliers or public houses will hire out glasses for a small sum (you also pay for any breakages). Stemmed glasses are for wine and, at a pinch, champagne, and squat tumblers for spirits. More exotic cocktails have their own shaped glasses: the more useful are tall tumblers for Collins and Pimms, and small stemmed glasses for Martinis.

Ice Start making ice for any party a couple of days ahead. Empty cubes from ice trays into a poly bag and store in the freezer. If you have a vacuum ice container, fill that up ready. Crush ice by whirling in a strong blender, or merely by beating with a rolling pin between 2 tea towels.

Decorative ice cubes In your ice-cube trays, you can freeze tiny sprigs of selected herbs – mint, say – or small whole raspberries or strawberries, which can enhance a cocktail. Or freeze orange or lemon juice – children love this in their 'cocktails'.

Cocktails It is best to limit the number of cocktails you serve at a party – a choice of 3 perhaps – and be sure you have all the necessary ingredients. Have ready the slices of lemon or lime (can be pre-cut and stored in the freezer), the maraschino cherries, and any mixers like tonic water, tomato juice or ginger ale should be chilled too if you've room in the fridge. Some cocktails benefit from being served in chilled glasses.

White wine This is a good drink for a summer party – and best for slimmers too! If serving with a meal, it traditionally accompanies fish and white meats – but there are no firm rules. Have whatever you enjoy. White wine should be chilled for 1-2 hours before serving (good wines for the shorter time). Too cold, and the flavour will be dulled.

Red wine Traditionally served with game and darker meats, but always ask the advice of your wine merchant if you're uncertain. Once opened a good red wine should stand for 2 hours (less good for 3) to bring it to room temperature and to allow it to breathe. Many good mature red wines which have sediment at the bottom will need decanting.

Other wine drinks Kir is Crème de Cassis with a chilled dry or sparkling white wine (Cardinal is Cassis and a light red). A good white wine cup is pleasant, and for a winter evening party, welcome guests with a warm mug of mulled red wine.

Choose the appropriate wine Serve Rioja with paella, Chianti with pasta, and Californian with hamburgers at a 4th of July barbecue.

Hangover cure Lots of black coffee, sweet tea, Coca-Cola can help the next day – healthier than the 'hair of the dog'. A Prairie Oyster is 1 raw egg, a dash of Tabasco, Worcestershire Sauce, and salt and pepper mixed: I haven't tried this, but the mere thought pulls me round! I swear by drinking lots of water before going to bed.

Simple eats Serve hot or cold, but must be small enough to be eaten in one hand.

Dips Mix curry powder, mango chutney juice, mustard and cream cheese; or avocado flesh, mayonnaise, lemon juice; or horseradish cream, mayonnaise and soured cream. Serve with carrot and celery sticks, pieces of cucumber and cauliflower florets.

Salted almonds Make your own by blanching whole shelled almonds in boiling water to remove skins. Then fry in oil and butter, drain and salt.

Scratchings Roast bacon rinds until crisp.

Baby quiches Make your favourite recipe in small tartlet tins. My favourites are spinach, ham and cheese, and chive and chervil.

Freezing

I have written many times about freezers and freezing. Below I offer a few more unusual tips and ways in which you might use your freezer.

Recording the contents I find a freezer record book makes heavy weather of freezing. I use a large write-on/wipe-off board on the kitchen wall. As packs are put in, I record them; as packs are taken out, I wipe them off. In this way I always know exactly what's there. (Have handy on your board the engineer's number – you may need it in an emergency!)

Improvise containers Don't throw away old yoghurt and margarine pots, particularly if you have a baby to feed. They hold just enough puréed veg or stewed fruit for one baby meal.

Colour coding Give a different colour to each category of food, and package them in coloured bags or use coloured ties, so that you see at a glance where the meat or fish is, etc.

Preventing accidents So that the freezer isn't accidentally switched off, cover the socket switch with a criss-cross of coloured tape.

Vegetables It is useful to have small packs of diced veg in store which can be added straight to stews and casseroles without defrosting.

Freezing tomatoes Just put ripe unskinned ones in a poly bag in the freezer. Take out what you need, and in 10 minutes they will have thawed a little, and skins will slip off easily. Use in casseroles only.

Chicken stock Pack carcasses in poly bags and store in the freezer until you have 2 or 3. Then crush the frozen brittle bones with a rolling pin and make stock. Because the bones are crushed, they take up less room in the pan, and make a more concentrated stock.

Flavoured ice cubes Buy tomato purée in cheaper larger cans and freeze in cubes for use in sauces.

Home-made soups and stocks Concentrated (boiled down), they take up less freezer space, and can be brought back to the right consistency by adding water, milk or cream when reheating. Freeze in ice cubes too, for your own 'stock cubes'.

Budget marmalade Never throw away squeezed lemon or grapefruit halves or orange peel. Freeze wrapped in clingfilm and use for marmalade when you've got enough.

Herb butters Freeze herb butters in waxed paper rolls for easy slicing. Use for herb breads or for topping grills or steaks. (Garlic butter doesn't freeze well.)

Croûtons Fry a whole loaf at once, drain and cool, then pack in poly bags. Taken out of freezer as required, they just need warming at the last minute.

Bread in the freezer Freeze cut loaves as well as uncut, so that a few slices only at a time can be used. Toast sliced frozen bread for a little longer than usual for fast toast. Remember that breadcrumbs freeze well, ready for instant use.

Fast defrosting of the freezer My husband always says 'Grasp the kettle and get on with it'! Defrosting is one of those jobs you put off, but no need – it's easy done first thing in the morning, and it can be completed in under an hour.

1. Fill your largest pan with water, and boil.
2. Switch off the freezer. Empty contents on to newspaper on the floor in a neat pile – icecream in the middle. Cover pile with old sleeping bags or rugs.
3. Open door or lid of freezer. Put a wad of newspaper on floor or base then put in the pan of just-off-the-boil water. Close lid or door.
4. Do another job in the house for 30 minutes.
5. Sort out the food into logical piles and replace in stacking wire baskets, the freezer drawers, boxes or large plastic bags. Colour code.
6. Open the freezer lid or door and remove pan of water. By now the ice will have thawed. Collect it up with a dustpan and brush. Mop up water with old towels, then wipe dry. Close lid or door. Switch on, and leave for 5 minutes.
7. Replace food in baskets, etc. Vow to keep the freezer tidy and to repeat this procedure every few months.

Super soups

Soups are nutritious, filling and warming, and are ideal for the first course of a meal, formal or informal, for a quick lunch accompanied by crusty bread, or for a snack on coming home from school or work. Home-made are best, and they're so easy.

Firstly stock For a rich brown stock, brown the bones in a hot oven before adding water and seasonings. Take care not to overdo it!

Bones for stock The best are beef, chicken or ham (delicious for pea soup). Only use lamb bones for Scotch Broth. Raw bones give the clearest and most intensely flavoured stock.

Storing stock Cool and chill in fridge, then remove any solidified fat. Meat stock will last for up to 4 days, but keep fish for 2 only.

Freezing stock Concentrated, so that it doesn't take up much space, it will keep for up to 2 months.

Vegetable water Always keep the water in which vegetables have been cooked for stocks and soups. Make sure it is not too salty, though.

Save cooked vegetables Keep putting leftover veg in a container in the freezer. When there's enough, use to make soup. Purée in processor or blender with stock, reheat and check seasoning.

Extra-nutritious soup Add pearl barley or soaked lentils, beans or dried bean and lentil mix (½ oz or 15 g per person). It not only adds to the food value, but tastes good and adds body to the soup.

Quick soup thickener Add a little instant potato powder at the end of cooking time. Especially good with a cauliflower or vegetable soup.

Soup too salty Thin down with stock then add grated potato or other root veg to absorb the salt. Do not add sugar to compensate!

For the best flavour Sauté or 'sweat' the onions or vegetables gently in butter for a while before adding the stock.

Simmer soups gently They should never be boiled rapidly or they will evaporate and reduce. If the veg are cut up small they will cook more quickly and can be added towards the end of cooking.

To avoid skin on soups Evaporation from the surface is the cause of skin, so keep soups covered with lid or foil. Skin is easily disposed of by liquidising.

Milk in soups Milk helps to enrich soups, but they tend to boil over easily, so *watch* them. Add milk after soup has been puréed and before it is reheated. The same applies to single cream. Add a swirl of whipped cream as a last-minute garnish.

Chilled soups Keep butter to a minimum, and be sure to skim off all the fat before chilling. The consistency should be of a thin pouring sauce as the soup will thicken as it cools.

Seasoning chilled soups They will need *more* seasoning when served cold.

Add colour to soups A pinch of paprika looks good on a pale-coloured soup, as does a sprinkling of chopped parsley or chives.

Add crunch to soups Tiny pieces of red or green pepper or small sprigs of cauliflower or anything else relevant adds textural interest to smooth soup.

Soup special Add a couple of tablespoons of sherry to home-made game soup or to the richer canned soups. It does something for shellfish soups too.

Croûtons Don't waste the crusts off bread. Cut into small cubes and fry in vegetable oil.

Melba toast Toast thin slices of crustless bread on both sides. Carefully split the slices through the centre and toast the uncooked sides momentarily (*do* watch them) until crisp.

Fishy things

Although Britain is surrounded by rich fishing waters, it can be difficult to buy good fresh fish in many parts of the country. If you happen to find a reliable fishmonger, treasure him.

Buying fresh fish Look for brightness. The eyes should be prominent, the gills red, and the scales sparkling. The body should be firm, and there should be a fresh smell. Try to cook the same day.

Freezing fishy things This is not usually advisable unless you have caught it yourself, or know its exact provenance. Fishmongers' fish may have been transported across country and may already have been frozen.

The advantages of fish Fish is quick to cook, so is useful when you're in a hurry. White fish is low in calories and rich in protein. Oily fish contains protein as well as Vitamin D, good for teeth and bones (in fact the only other real 'source' of D is sunshine).

The versatility of fish Fish is as versatile as meat, if not more so. Smoked fish pâtés freeze better than meat, and make an easy starter; fillets of fish can be used in many delicious starter or main course dishes; fish makes wonderful soups, pies or stews; it can be barbecued, made into fish cakes, grilled as steaks or whole, served for breakfast (a protein-rich start to the day), deep-fried in a tasty coating for fish and chips or – further up the culinary scale – as scampi. And it is no surprise that some of the most luxurious and coveted foods of the world – caviar and the best Scotch smoked salmon, for instance – are fishy things.

Slippery fish To stop fish from slipping while handling it, put some salt on your fingers.

Skinning a fillet Hold the fish by the tail. Skin from the tail to the head with quick, short, sawing strokes, keeping the edge of the blade close to the surface of the skin so that no flesh is lost.

Fiddly bones When you can't pull out the bones from raw fish with your fingers, use an old pair of eyebrow tweezers which grip the bones well.

Coating fish Place seasoned flour in a plastic bag then add the fish and give it a good shake. The fish is evenly coated and there is no mess. An inexpensive coating is a mixture of flour and milk, then good breadcrumbs. If using egg for the liquid for the coating, spin it out by adding 1 tablespoon oil.

Cooking fish The best methods are poaching (*not* boiling), steaming (traditionally good for invalids), grilling, frying or deep-frying in batter. Most fish will lose its transparent look and turn milky – white when cooked (in about 5-10 minutes). Always check for done-ness at the thickest part near the bone. Fish cooks very quickly, and is easily spoiled if the temperature is too fierce or the cooking time too long.

Thawing fish in a hurry Put frozen fish or fillets in a polythene bag then immerse in cold water (thus not losing any flavour).

Buying shellfish Divided into molluscs (mussels, oysters, winkles, whelks and cockles), and crustaceans (shrimps, prawns, crabs, lobsters), shellfish are usually sold cooked – with the exception of oysters and mussels. Choose those that look fresh and clean; in the case of molluscs, the shells should be tightly closed (discard or refuse to buy open ones).

Thawing shellfish Thaw commercially frozen shellfish carefully and completely, and then use as soon as possible. Packets of prawns can contain an amazing proportion of water to prawns, so make doubly sure to get rid of all the liquid.

Mussels Wash live mussels several times to remove sand and scrub off any beard. To make them open, put in a pan with a little water (or wine and flavourings) and cook quickly, covered, for about 5 minutes until shells open. Any that are still closed should be thrown away.

Use shellfish imaginatively Barbecue or curry spice prawns; make a crab sauce to accompany cod or haddock; put scallops or oysters into a classic fish pie; add shrimps to white fish dishes.

Meaty things

Like the elusive fishmonger, a good butcher is worth his weight in gold. Make friends with him, ask his advice, and more than likely he will be able to point you towards things of good value.

How to recognise good beef The meat should be firm to the touch. The lean should have a bright red colour with a brownish tinge, and contain small flecks of fat (to keep it moist during cooking). The fat should be creamy in colour (although it varies), and there should be little fat or gristle on prime cuts.

How to recognise good lamb The flesh of a young lamb (often with a blue tinge to the knuckle bone) should be light pink; that of an older animal is darker. The fat should be creamy white (yellowish or brittle white fat indicates elderly meat or too long in the freezer), and a joint should be plump with a good layer of covering fat on legs and shoulders.

How to recognise good pork Young animals will have little gristle and the flesh will be pink in colour; older animals have darker and coarser flesh. Grey, soft or oily fat is a sign of poor quality, and a piece of pork should never feel wet to the touch.

Veal This accounts for only 4 per cent of the meat sold in this country, partly because of its cost. For cheaper substitute escalopes, beat chicken or turkey breasts or slices of pork tenderloin between polythene, and then cook as per your favourite veal recipe.

Offal Most commonly available offal is cheap and very nutritious. Pregnant and nursing mothers, indeed *all* of us, should have liver, for instance, once a week as it is so full of iron. A nice way of using calf's (if you can afford it) or lamb's liver is to cut it into strips, dip in seasoned flour, and cook as for your favourite stroganoff recipe.

Buying meat The best days to buy are Tuesday, Wednesday and Thursday (on Mondays they'll be restocking, and Fridays and Saturdays are always so busy).

Special cuts If you want your butcher to crown, roll or bone your meat, order it in advance; *don't* hold up the queue on Saturday morning.

Buying meat in bulk This can be a great saving if there is a special offer and you have a freezer large enough. But a whole beast or even half *can* incorporate cuts that no-one in the family will ever consider eating – like scrag, offal, heads and tails – so is it worth it?

Storing meat If meat is to be kept in the fridge, don't cut it up small or mince it – it will last better in one piece.

Frying meat Wet meat doesn't brown quickly, so rinsed or thawed cuts should be patted dry with absorbent paper before frying. Fry cubed meat for casseroles quickly to seal it, as this holds the flavour in. When frying a steak, be sure to heat the pan really well first (a non-stick one is best as you'll need little or no fat).

Grilling meat Snip the fat on chops, steaks and bacon to prevent them curling up during cooking (the fat cooks and shrivels faster than the lean). Heat the grill well beforehand for steaks.

Grilling bacon Overlap back rashers like roof tiles – this way the fat on top of the lean becomes crisp and the lean remains moist.

Barbecuing meat Marinate it well before cooking as this improves the flavour and tenderises cheaper cuts. For the simplest of marinades, mix 3 tablespoons oil, 1 tablespoon vinegar, a crushed clove garlic, and a small chopped onion. Blend well with up to 2 lb (900 g) meat in cubes (for kebabs), slices, chops or steaks, then cover and keep in the fridge for 1–2 days.

Boiling bacon or ham First bring to the boil then simmer gently, and add a peeled onion and a bay leaf. This simmering, covered, means less shrinkage. Allow 20 minutes per lb (450 g), and 20 minutes over for small joints. For joints over 5 lb (2.25 kg) allow 15 minutes to the lb (450 g). Leave to cool in the cooking water which will ensure maximum moisture and tenderness.

Meat spinners

Meat is probably the most expensive item in the family budget, and everyone would like to spin a little out to feed a lot. This is also relevant to emergency entertaining – how to feed those unexpected guests when all you've got is 2 chops.

The secret of success Perhaps the most basic is to have a well-stocked store cupboard, fridge and freezer. Good meat spinners from the store cupboard are pasta, rice, pastry mixes, canned or dried beans, cans of ham, vegetables like sweetcorn and petits pois. From the fridge could come most of the ingredients for a substantial meat salad, and from the freezer could come the pizza bases, pastry flan cases, pancakes and frozen veg.

Serve another course first The classic Yorkshire way of making the Sunday roast beef go further was to serve the pudding separately with gravy. After this, you were supposed to need less of the expensive meat! Apply the same principle by serving a good economical thick soup first.

Beanfeast A small amount of meat can still make a substantial – and nutritious – casserole if you add beans. The choice now available in health-food shops, delis and larger supermarkets is enormous, and they're full of protein. They must be soaked overnight in cold water then drained and brought to the boil (if using red kidney beans, boil for at least 10 minutes to get rid of toxins). Simmer until tender in the stew or casserole. Allow about ½ oz (15 g) raw beans per person. Season towards end of cooking period to prevent beans becoming tough. If an emergency, add a can of beans towards the end of cooking.

Dumplings Very easy to make and add to the bulk as well as look of a casserole. Just mix 4 oz (110 g) self-raising flour, 1 teaspoon baking powder, 2 oz (50 g) suet, salt and pepper with about 2 tablespoons milk to form a soft dough. Roll into 6–8 balls and put on top of the meat for the last 40 minutes of cooking. To give variety, add chopped parsley or other herbs or, for beef, a little grated horseradish as well.

Gardener's meat pie Cut the meat by half and more than double the amount of vegetables. A good trick is to cut the meat into smaller cubes and add a good variety of vegetables – but do go easy on the more strongly flavoured like swede, parsnip and turnip.

Expanding mince Minced meat is perhaps the most versatile of meats that can be made to go further. For Scotch mince, add 1 tablespoon porridge oats per 1 lb (450 g) of meat. For a shepherd's pie expand a little with a couple of slices of brown bread crumbled into the meat and gravy. You could also add some cooked rice (1 part rice to 5 parts mince), or some soya granules. For tang, add 1 coarsely grated cooking apple per 8 oz (225 g) meat before cooking.

Meatballs Mix breadcrumbs from 3–4 slices white bread into 1 lb (450 g) mince, with seasonings and flavourings to taste – grated Parmesan cheese, chopped or dried herbs, finely chopped bacon or onion – and an egg to bind. Form into small balls and fry in hot fat, turning to brown on all sides. Serve with an instant store-cupboard tomato sauce, plus rice or noodles.

Expand a meal for 2 to feed 4 2 steaks can be minced and made into meatballs, or the steaks or pork chops for 2 can be cut into chunks and grilled on skewers as kebabs for 4 – add chunks of bacon, cheese, onion, apple and mushrooms.

Making sausage rolls Add 1 packet of sage and onion stuffing mix, made up, to each 1 lb (450 g) sausagemeat. It makes the meat go further.

Add pastry A small amount of meat can feed more if topped, surrounded, or encased by pastry. Think of Cornish pasties, plate meat pies, chops and beef en croûte (try pork fillet, it's cheaper).

Leftover meat Can be minced, finely chopped or sliced for use in a variety of ways. Try chicken or turkey in a white sauce with cubes of ham and fried button mushrooms; or in a cheese sauce as the filling for pancakes (from the freezer?) or an omelette; or as the topping for a pizza or quiche. Mix with cream, garlic, herbs for pasta sauces, or combine with other ingredients to stuff veg.

Meat salads Add hard-boiled eggs, cooked veg, canned veg, onions, potatoes, mayonnaise.

Roasting

Strictly speaking what we call roasting today isn't roasting – which is cooking in a current of air in front of or over a fierce glowing heat (a rôtisserie or spit roaster, for instance). Enclosing a joint in an oven in dry heat is actually baking.

Meat roasting times and temperatures These are approximate, and for the average roast of about 3–5 lb (1.3–2.2 kg). Temperature for quick roasting is 425°F/220°C/Gas 7, for slow roasting, 325°F/160°C/Gas 3. Times are per lb (450 g).

Meat	Quick roast at high temp.	Slow roast at low temp.
Beef	15 mins + 15 (rare)	25 + 25 (well done)
Lamb/mutton	20 mins + 20	30 mins + 30
Pork	25 mins + 25	35 mins + 35 mins at high for crackling
Chicken/duck	15 mins + 15	25 mins + 25
Goose/turkey	15 mins + 15	25 mins + 25

Emulate the basics of spit-roasting Start a joint roasting by putting into a very hot oven for a few minutes to seal the meat (to keep in moisture, flavour and goodness), then cook at relevant lower temperature in normal way.

Never over-cook a joint again Use a roasting meat thermometer, which specifies ideal inner temperatures for beef, pork, lamb etc.

To lift a heavy cooked joint Put 2 strips of treble thickness foil at right angles under the joint in tin *before* cooking. Lift out after cooking, and put tin on a firm surface on a damp dishcloth to prevent slipping. Beware of hot, dripping juices.

For perfect roast potatoes Heat the oven to 425°F/220°C/Gas 7. Peel potatoes, cut into even-sized pieces, and par-boil for 3 minutes. Drain well. Heat vegetable oil in tin before roasting par-boiled potatoes, near the top of the oven, for about 1½ hours, or until golden brown and wonderfully crispy.

Still room in the roasting tin? Roast onions with lamb (about 1 hour), apples beside pork and par-boiled parsnips with beef (about 30 minutes).

Thicker gravy When making batter for Yorkshire pudding, save a drop and mix it into the gravy to thicken it and give it a lovely texture.

For a delicious gravy Roast meat on a bed of chopped onions and carrots. The sugar in the veg caramelises, and makes a wonderful basis for the gravy.

Lean roast beef For maximum flavour, bard a lean cut – as the French do – with the right fat, so that it can baste itself during cooking. Either cover with a slice of fat, or sew strips through (for fillet).

Pot-roasting beef For an economical slow beef roast, cook de-fatted, boned and rolled brisket in a roasting tin with some onions and carrots, covered with 1 pt (550 ml) stock, and foil. Allow 30 minutes at the high temperature, then lower to 300°F/150°C/Gas 2 for 50 minutes per lb (450 g). It's lovely cold, too.

Crisp pork crackling Score fat finely then brush with oil or a butter paper and sprinkle with salt. Cook high at first or for last ½ hour, until fat crisps and bubbles.

Crispy roast lamb Spread skin with redcurrant or mint jelly, then sprinkle with rosemary and roast in usual way. Garlic is also good when rubbed into the fat of lamb before roasting.

Make roast duck go further Roast a boned piece of belly pork, skin scored, alongside the duck. Serve with the duck, and no one will notice the difference. (A tip from a farmer's wife in Devon where we spent early holidays with the kids.)

Roast chicken Make a herb butter by mixing 2 oz (50 g) butter with 1 tablespoon freshly chopped herbs. Loosen skin from meat with fingers, starting at top of the breast, then spread butter between flesh and skin, reaching right down to thighs. Roast in the usual way.

To carve a turkey easily Remove wishbone before cooking by lifting skin from neck end, and running a sharp knife along each side of the bone. For those who enjoy pulling the wishbone, cook it alongside the bird.

Know your bird

Poultry and winged game, although superficially similar – they're all birds – are in fact very different when it comes to preparation and cooking. As with meat, it pays to get to know your poulterer or butcher, so that you buy wisely.

Thawing chickens and small birds Thaw *completely* before cooking, overnight at room temperature on a plate in a place away from pets, covered with a meat-guard or something similar, or in a closed ventilated cupboard. Remember to remove neck, giblets and any loose fat before cooking.

To test when birds are cooked Pierce the thickest part of the thigh with a skewer. If clear juices run, the bird is cooked; if pink, continue cooking until clear.

How to carve poultry Set bird on non-slip surface like a wooden board. Allow to rest for 10 minutes before carving so that juices settle, and the meat becomes firmer. This also gives you plenty of time to make your gravy.

Chicken This must be the most popular and versatile of birds, as its mild but lovely flavour can be utilised in so many ways: roasted, braised, barbecued, in pies, curries, and cold in salads.

Grilling chicken Poussins – young chickens up to 6 weeks old – are very tender. Allow 1 bird per person then snip through backbone with scissors. Flatten, fix with 2 skewers, then grill.

Boiling fowl These are old laying hens and are best used in casseroles as they need a long slow cooking time. They have a good flavour but expect them to be fatty. Simmer in water with flavourings; use the flesh for something like salad or a fricassee, and the stock for soup (remove fat first, and use for cooking).

Stuffing chicken, duck and turkey Stuff neck cavity of chickens and turkeys; it cooks more quickly and is easier to carve. Cook stuffing for duck separately as duck is very greasy and its nice to have that baked crispiness.

Duck fat To roast out, prick the duck skin all over then rub with salt. Decant fat during roasting and use for frying potatoes – the taste is quite delicious.

Choosing a fresh turkey Look for a bird whose breast is broad in proportion to its length, which means there is plenty of white meat. Remember you will be paying for an undrawn bird, the head, feet etc (which amounts to about 3 lb or over a kilo in a large bird).

Defrosting a turkey Do this at room temperature.

6–8 lb (2.7–3.6 kg)	13–18 hours
8–12 lb (3.6–5.4 kg)	18–24 hours
12–16 lb (5.4–7.2 kg)	24–26 hours
16–20 lb (7.2–9 kg)	26–28 hours
20–24 lb (9–10.8 kg)	28–30 hours

Microwave thawing For a 12–16 lb (5.4–7.2 kg) turkey, begin defrosting in wrapper for 15 minutes. Stand 15 minutes. Turn over and uncover. Cover with clingfilm. Defrost 10 minutes. Stand 1–1½ hours if not completely defrosted. Alternate defrosting and standing times to prevent excess heating of outside of bird. Remove giblets soonest.

Cooking your goose At its best from October to Christmas, a 10 lb (4.5 kg) oven-ready bird will serve 8. As it's very fatty, roast on a rack in a tin, or *on* the oven rack, with a tin underneath to catch the fat. Roast stuffing separately (as with duck), and use delicious fat, rendered, for sautéing, basting, or for the topping of a pâté.

Game birds All must be hung in a cool draughty place, to tenderise the bird and add flavour. Time varies according to the weather and the size of bird. I usually hang pheasants for about 7 days. Young birds are best roasted and old birds should be marinated and casseroled, or made into puddings, pies or pâtés.

Roasting poultry Most birds – excepting only the most fatty, like duck or goose – require barding – fat or streaky bacon over the top. If browning too quickly, cover with foil, but remove for last 15 minutes or so of cooking time.

Rotating poultry during roasting Start the bird off on one side, then turn it over to the other, then roast for the longest time with breast up. This ensures juices moisten all sides.

Puddings

Almost everyone loves puddings (except perhaps those of us who need to lose a little weight), and it's understandable when one thinks of the good things that go into them – fruit, cream and eggs. Choose the recipe according to season and other accompanying courses for a good finish to a meal.

Think ahead Make more than enough rice pudding and use leftovers for pear Condé or Connaught rice the next day. Any simple stewed fruit can be made into a fool later with cream. Make enough mousse to serve today, plus several small dishes to go into the freezer. Keep back some fruit salad to make trifle.

Boiling puddings Stand the pudding in a pan on a metal jam-jar lid, and top up with water. This stops contact with the pan and the pudding will cook more evenly.

Steaming puddings Add a little vinegar to the water to prevent the pan turning black. Never let the pan boil dry.

A marvellous tip . . . When boiling or steaming puddings, put a few glass marbles in the bottom of the double pan. They will rattle and warn that the pan has boiled dry.

To turn out a pudding Lift the basin out of the steamer and remove covering. Leave to cool for about 5 minutes until shrunk slightly, then loosen around sides to let in air. Put a dish over the basin and turn upside down. If basin was well-greased it should come out easily. This can be done ahead of time, and the basin left sitting on the pudding to keep it warm.

Baked custards Bake egg custards, caramel custards and custards for crème brûlées in a bain marie with a folded newspaper in the bottom. This prevents direct contact with heat so the custard won't form bubbles.

Setting jelly quickly Melt the jelly cubes in only a small amount of hot water and make up the rest with cold water and ice-cubes, or the drained juice of canned fruit if using.

To dissolve gelatine Sprinkle 1 packet (½ oz or 15 g) gelatine over 3 tablespoons cold water in a cup or small bowl, allow to stand for 5 minutes to form a sponge, then stand cup or bowl over a pan of simmering water until gelatine has dissolved and liquid is clear. Cool a little before mixing with other ingredients, as it is likely to go stringy. This amount should set about 1 pt (550 ml) liquid.

To unmould a mousse dessert Start by loosening the edge of the mould with the tip of a knife blade dipped in hot water. Then dip the mould up to the rim in a bowl of hand-hot water (if mould is thick china or ovenglass, use almost boiling water as heat goes through more slowly). Put a serving plate over top of mould then turn over. The mousse should come out easily (especially if mould was brushed first with vegetable oil).

For the best flavour Allow mousses to stand at room temperature for an hour before serving. The consistency as well as the flavour is much improved.

Quick setting glaze Put a fruit flan case in the freezer for 20 minutes before putting on the glaze – which then sets straightaway.

Sponge flan lining When filling a sponge flan case with fruit, line it first with a little melted cooking chocolate. Let it set and then arrange fruit on top. The chocolate stops the sponge going soggy – *delicious* with sliced bananas.

Good topping for icecream Heat through some apricot or cherry jam and add a little apricot brandy to apricot, or Kirsch to the cherry.

No time to make brandy or rum butter? Flavour whipped double cream with brandy or rum to go with the Christmas pudding – or anything!

To crush digestive biscuits Put into a clean poly bag and roll firmly with a rolling pin, or use a double thickness of poly bags and *stand* on them until crushed! Very quick and easy.

Vegetables

Always buy the best in season – don't be tempted, for example, to buy courgettes at Christmas! – and use up as soon as possible (Vitamin C is lost in storage). Try to serve a variety of fresh vegetables at each meal, and at least a couple of 'vegetarian' meals per week – for both economy and health.

Add colour If the main course has a white sauce, choose the accompanying vegetables to offer contrast – tomatoes for red, for example, and the green of beans or peas. Snip chives or parsley over white or pale veg such as celeriac, cauliflower, potatoes etc. Toasted or fried breadcrumbs can add texture as well as colour.

Add flavour Never forget that some vegetables can taste too strong for some meats. A delicately flavoured fish would be swamped by the robustness of parsnip, for instance (asparagus would be a better accompaniment).

Add texture Serve plain boiled vegetables with a casserole; use puréed vegetables and sauces with dry meats.

Add variety Make vegetables a little more exciting by mixing them together. If there is a shortage of courgettes, say, then use peas to spin them out. Carrots, sliced or in sticks, can be added to almost anything else, as can tomatoes. The classic vegetable bake is ratatouille, and mushrooms, beans, sprigs of broccoli, mangetouts, cauliflower, peas can all be happily intermingled in one splendidly colourful dish.

Stir-fried vegetables Stir-frying is a fast and healthy way of cooking vegetables. Very little fat is used, no water (to leach out goodness), and they can be easily and quickly cooked to required crispness in a matter of minutes. Cut all vegetables to approximately the same size. Pieces should be small to ensure quick and even cooking.

Golden purées Puréed vegetables can be mixed too for taste and colour. Cooked swede and carrot can be puréed together, with some butter and freshly ground black pepper. Celeriac and potato make another excellent purée. Sprinkle with chopped herbs for colour, nuts for texture.

Vegetables as starters Fairly inexpensive and very healthy. Serve cold leeks in vinaigrette, asparagus (in season, of course), globe artichokes, avocado with a special or simple stuffing, corn on the cob, stuffed mushroom caps, mushrooms in a sauce, or a simple vegetable soup.

Stuffed vegetables Many can be topped or filled with a tasty stuffing for a hearty meal or an interesting starter – mushrooms, peppers, tomatoes, aubergines, marrows, onions – even the humble baked potato can be 'stuffed' with a soufflé mix for a special occasion.

For easy peeling Carrots can be blanched for a few minutes, and then the skins will scrape off easily. Peppers and tomatoes can be held over a flame until skin splits and peels off (tomatoes can also be put in boiling water for a few seconds). Many potato varieties and Jerusalem artichokes are better scraped of peel *after* cooking.

Cooking green vegetables The golden rules are that if it grows above ground, cook with the lid off (in a pan of as little water as is practicable), and lid on for below-ground veg. Cook cauliflower and cabbage with the window open as the smell tends to linger!

Mushrooms Never peel cultivated mushrooms as much of the flavour and goodness lies in or just under the skin. Wipe with a damp cloth only. Store dry in the fridge, loosely covered with clingfilm, and use as soon as possible.

Beetroot Leave both the root and a few inches of the stem end on before boiling. If either is cut away, the beetroot 'bleeds' into the water and loses its colour. To stop your fingers from getting stained when slicing beetroot, slice in an egg slicer.

Speed up baked potatoes To cut the time by 20 minutes, boil the potatoes for 10 minutes in their skins before putting in the oven. To cut time by 10 minutes, insert metal skewers, which conduct the heat right into the potato.

Golden fried onions Add a teaspoon caster sugar when frying; this helps the onions become a golden colour quickly.

Chopping onions with no tears Keep the cut side of the onion towards the board, and don't lean over. Other remedies include running cold water, and keeping a stainless steel spoon in your mouth!

Salads

A salad may be served as a course in its own right, or may complement another dish; after a home-made soup, it makes a good simple lunch; served in individual dishes with an interesting dressing, it can be a good starter. The secrets are variety, crispness, freshness and look.

Keeping salad leaves There are all sorts – Cos, round, iceberg, Webbs, Chinese leaves, lamb's lettuce, endive, and the glamorous radicchio. Take off any tatty outside leaves, then dunk remaining head up and down in a bowl of icy, slightly salty water. Shake gently but well and store in a polythene bag in the fridge. If fridge is full, will keep well in a cool place in a large heavy saucepan.

Keeping watercress Take off elastic band or string, and dunk bunch in cool, slightly salted water, removing any yellow leaves. Gather bunch together again, and put heads down in a jug of water until needed. Store in a cool place.

Cabbage and chicory Wrap whole or part in clingfilm and keep in the fridge.

Peppers and fennel Keep in the salad or 'crisper' drawer in the fridge. Or store in a loosely folded-over polythene bag in the fridge (not a sealed bag, as they can go soggy).

Parsley and leafy herbs Ideally pick or buy with the stalks on. Wash and shake bunch dry, holding stalks together, then put in polythene bag. Do not seal, just fold over, and keep in fridge.

Cucumber Leave in polythene sleeve if it has one, or wrap in clingfilm and store in fridge.

Vegetable salads Never forget that cold cooked vegetables – whether specially cooked or leftover – can make splendid salads. Toss them in French dressing and scatter with freshly chopped parsley. Add cold crisp chunks of bacon or ham, and a few nuts perhaps.

Winter salads Give more interest by adding finely shredded Brussels sprouts or leeks. Use fairly sparingly, though, as they have strong flavours raw.

Less usual salads Many vegetables normally eaten cooked can be used happily raw in salads – slices of mushroom, for instance, or washed spinach leaves (with a few croûtons, crushed garlic, and chunks of crispy bacon).

Make a main-meal salad Add sliced cold chicken or other cold meats to a vegetable salad. Or add strips of Cheddar or Gruyère cheese.

For a subtle onion flavour Raw onion can be too strong in many salads (Spanish are milder), so for just a hint, squeeze some onion in your garlic press and add the juice to the salad dressing.

For a quick dressing Put equal quantities of oil and vinegar with a little sugar, a dash of curry powder or mustard, and seasoning in a screwtop jar and shake vigorously until all is mixed.

Oils Olive is considered the luxury salad oil, but a drop of walnut 'lifts' a less tasty oil.

Vinegars Malt vinegar is too harsh, so use wine (red or white), cider or home-made or bought herb vinegars. Lemon juice can be used as well for a milder flavour.

Dressing the salad Never pour dressing over a green salad in advance as it causes the leaves to wilt. Put dressing in a bowl with the chunky ingredients – pepper, cucumber, tomatoes and onion – then top with green salad leaves. Toss just before serving.

Keeping the colour Retain the colour of apple or avocado (or any vegetable that changes colour when cut) by adding them directly to the oil and vinegar dressing for the salad.

Nuts Nuts give crunchiness when added to salads: a few flaked almonds make all the difference to a rice salad, as do walnuts to a Waldorf salad. Try pine kernels for an interesting flavour too.

Vary your dressings A French dressing can have added garlic, herbs, curry powder, chives or tomato. A mayonnaise, bought or home-made, can be flavoured with herbs, tomato or garlic.

Getting fruity

Fruit is everywhere, and never before has it been so popular. Now available from all over the world as well as from our own orchards and greenhouses, we have become familiar with many fruits we could only read about a generation ago. Buy it at its best, at its freshest, for health and pleasure.

All the year round Due to modern methods of cultivation and transportation, many fruits are now available all year round. By preserving or freezing, other fruits – raspberries, for instance – can have their 'season' extended to bring delight to a Christmas meal, for instance. Buy fruit when it is plentiful and cheap – or harvest your own – and freeze it for the rest of the year.

Over-ripe fruit Never turn these down if they're cheaper. Use over-ripe bananas for icecream or banana cake; strawberries, raspberries etc for making purées, mousses etc. Don't be tempted to use in jams as you will be very disappointed in the result. Use fruit in peak condition.

Use fruit imaginatively Fruit can be eaten raw, can be cooked in pies, flans etc, and made into delicious desserts of all kinds – but it can also add taste, texture and colour to many savoury dishes: try apricot halves filled with mint jelly to accompany cold lamb, or peach halves filled with chutney or pineapple slices topped with coleslaw with ham or pork; bake apples to accompany roast pork, or chop and braise with red cabbage; serve a cherry sauce with duck, etc.

Fruit as garnish A thin slice of fried apple looks wonderful atop a curried apple soup or with a hearty fried breakfast; lemon butterflies (or lime or orange) would beautify almost anything; frosted cherries or grapes decorate savoury as well as sweet dishes; and slices of bright green kiwi fruit enliven any plate.

Fruit salads Fruit salads look their best when prepared and presented in clear glass bowls. Cheer up an everyday fruit salad by adding exotics such as sliced mango or kiwi fruit.

Buying and storing lemons Buy thin-skinned ones – they contain more juice – and store in a polythene bag in the fridge.

Lemon juice To get maximum juice, it helps if lemon is warm, or at least at kitchen temperature. If you only need a few drops, pierce lemon with a knitting needle instead of cutting in half. Remember to use it up quickly. If you have a microwave, cut lemon in half, put cut sides on a plate, and switch on for a few moments. The juice will be plentiful.

Lemon juice as bleach Rub stained fingertips with a used lemon shell; similarly lemon juice will get rid of onion or fishy smells on hands.

Grated lemon If you've grated the peel for a recipe and are left with a bald lemon, wrap in clingfilm and store in fridge for juice later.

Currants To quickly remove the stems, hold stem and run fork down to separate the currants.

Gooseberries Top and tail with scissors. No need to if making a fool; cook all together then sieve.

Apple sauce For a bright green colour and a full flavour, cook cut-up apples without peeling or coring, then sieve them – you'll get more purée for your money!

Prevent apples from turning brown If you are using several, drop the prepared apples in a bowl of salted water (1 tablespoon salt to 1 pint or 550 ml water). Rinse before using.

Sloes for sloe gin Instead of pricking each one laboriously with a hat pin, rub handfuls against the coarse side of a grater to pierce them. (Do not be over-vigorous in this.)

Fruit syrups I now rarely make these for fruit salads. I find that if you layer the fruit with caster sugar the day before, the fruits make their own syrup which can then be flavoured with liqueur or lemon juice to taste. Easy and delicious.

Fruit drinks Make your own Vitamin C-rich blackcurrant drink by stewing 1 lb (450 g) fruit with ½ pint (300 ml) water until tender. Sieve, add sugar, store in fridge and dilute to taste. Make fresh fruit squashes with oranges; and, of course, old-fashioned still lemonade from lemon.

Eggs and dairy

Eggs and dairy produce like milk, cream and cheese were once thought of indisputably as good for everyone. Even though doubts are now expressed about fats and cholesterol contained in them, they still remain fairly inexpensive, good to eat, and good to cook with. Use them sparingly perhaps, but for some methods or recipes they're absolutely essential!

Storing eggs Store in a cool place, larder or refrigerator, pointed end down. If kept in the fridge, take them out and let them reach room temperature before use (vital for meringues).

To tell if eggs are fresh Place in a bowl of water. Really fresh eggs will hug the bottom, less fresh will bob up a bit, and old and stale will float!

Eggs are porous Keep them away from other strong smelling foods like kippers or cheese, and any that you have had to wash, use up immediately.

Leftover yolks Store in the fridge in a small container. Float a dessertspoon of water over top to prevent a skin forming, and cover with clingfilm. Mark with waterproof pen the number of yolks in the container. Use within 1 week, for mayonnaise, lemon curd, hollandaise, to enrich sauces, or simply add to scrambled eggs.

Leftover whites Store in a container in the fridge. Label as above. Use within 3 weeks. If you lose count of how many are in the container, 4 egg whites are about ¼ pt (150 ml). Use for meringues, soufflés, soufflé toppings, pancakes, omelettes etc. Egg whites can be frozen for up to 6 months in an airtight container.

Crack-free boiled eggs Choose eggs at room temperature rather than from the fridge and pierce with a pin or egg piercer at the pointed end. If the egg cracks while boiling, some salt added to the water will prevent the white from becoming too messy.

Boiling a cracked egg If that is all that is available, it can still be used. Wrap tightly in foil then boil in the usual way.

Leaving a note for the milkman Put it in a poly bag and leave rolled inside the top of the bottle. The note will keep dry and intact in all kinds of weather.

Storing milk in the fridge Always put today's milk at the back of the fridge and open yesterday's, then it is easy to see which should be used first.

Prevent milk boiling over Watch the pan, and if about to boil over, remove quickly and firmly put down on a cold surface (a stainless steel draining board, for example). The bang and the cold surface will make the milk sink quickly.

Freshly soured milk Don't throw it away, use for making scones.

Cream types These are determined by fat content, each with a specified minimum. Double cream has 48% minimum, whips well and floats perfectly on Irish coffee. Whipping cream has 30% and whips well to a light volume. Single cream has an 18% minimum, does not whip, but is good to add to soups and sauces. Half cream has 12%, and is thin, delicious with fruit.

Soured cream This is single cream which has been soured commercially with a lactic culture. It has a soft texture with a sharp refreshing taste, and is delicious on baked potatoes. If unavailable, sour fresh single cream by adding lemon juice.

To stretch cream Use equal quantities of single and double, and whisk in a little caster sugar. Alternatively, whip a small carton of double until thick and fold in 2 egg whites stiffly whisked with a little caster sugar.

Storing cheese Keep in a loosely folded polythene bag in the fridge, and take out an hour before needed to develop its flavour at room temperature.

Freezing cheese Hard cheese will go crumbly after 3 weeks in the freezer, so it's best used for cooking. Rich soft cheeses like Brie, Camembert and Stilton freeze well wrapped in foil.

Grated cheese Grate more than you need and store in fridge or freezer. Saves time and energy!

No hard cheese for grating? Use semi-soft cheese and cut into small cubes. Melts as quickly.

Rice and pasta

The staple foods of a huge proportion of the world's population. Rice, probably the single most important food source, supports the cultures of China, Japan, India, South-West Asia, and large areas of the Middle East. Pasta isn't purely Italian either: varieties turn up in the cuisines of Russia, Thailand, China, Japan and Hungary.

Long-grain rice 4–5 times as long as it's wide, and when cooked, the grains are separate and fluffy. Aromatic rice is a type of long grain.

Brown rice The least processed, therefore to many the best. It has a nut-like flavour, and when cooked remains slightly crunchy. Takes twice as long to cook as white rice.

Par-boiled rice Treated before milling. The grain is soaked, steamed, dried, then milled to remove outer hull, which hardens the grain, making it extra separate and fluffy after cooking. (See packet for absorption cooking method.)

Pre-cooked rice This has been milled, cooked and dried. Package instructions should be followed carefully as brands will differ.

White or polished rice The most common form, usually from America. The outer husk is removed, and the layers of bran milled away until the grain is white.

Types of rice The best type of rice for an Italian risotto is arborio, or cristallo (a par-boiled arborio), and Basmati is vital for good curries.

How much rice to use Use one cup or mug to measure both rice and water. Fill right to the brim, and use double liquid to rice – or 2 cups liquid to 1 cup rice. A mug or cup of uncooked rice will produce about 4 cups cooked, so 8 oz (225 g) raw will happily serve 3–4 people as accompaniment.

Washing rice Wash only unrefined or brown rice in cold water before cooking. This removes loose starch and prevents it sticking.

Cooking rice Place water in pan and bring to the boil. Add salt and rice and cover tightly. Reduce heat, and simmer gently for about 15–20 minutes.

Cooking rice in the oven Use boiling water. Combine measured rice and water in a casserole and stir. Cover and cook at 350°F/180°C/Gas 4 for 25–30 minutes.

To reheat rice Put in a covered pan with a few tablespoons water and heat gently. Shake the pan occasionally and rice will become fluffy again.

Instant savoury rice Add flavourings and frozen mixed veg to boiled rice a few minutes before end of cooking. Much cheaper than ready-mixed packs.

Cooking pasta Always cook in salted boiling water, but there are now so many types that it's difficult to be exact about timing. The following is a rough guide for dry pasta – check on the packet.

Lasagne about 12–15 minutes
Macaroni about 15 minutes
Spaghetti about 10–12 minutes
Tagliatelle about 8–10 minutes

How much pasta to use A 1 lb (450 g) packet of spaghetti will serve 4–6 people.

Cooking spaghetti Use the largest pot you have, and bring its full capacity of water to the boil. Add salt, then the pasta, coiling it in as the hot water softens it. Keep it boiling and moving until the strands are all separate. To test for doneness, lift a strand out and bite – it should be tender but with a slight bite in the middle. When done, add 1 cup cold water to stop cooking without chilling pasta. Drain in a colander.

Adding oil to pasta water This stops the pasta sticking together when drained.

Lasagne When cooked, run cold water into pot and move sheets around in water until separate. Cool in water, then drain on teatowels. Layer with béchamel and ragú sauces, or why not try smoked fish in an onion sauce? The precooked varieties now available can be layered dry with sauces.

Adding pasta Very small shapes make good soup thickeners, as do shapes added to a runny casserole 30 minutes before end of cooking time.

Pastry

Pastry is one of those things that many cooks dread making, while as many can prepare it happily in a moment with no qualms at all. For success every time, there are a lot of rules to remember, but once they're mastered, pastry shouldn't present any problem at all.

The basic secret Cold hands, chilled fat, cold (even iced) water, and a cool rolling-out surface (marble is the best). *Air* trapped in the making of the dough will expand more if cold, thus making pastry rise well and become light.

The importance of air All pastries depend on air as above. Trap it and retain it in your dough by sieving the flour from a height, using a large mixing bowl, cutting in small pieces of fat with a knife, lifting your hands well above the bowl when rubbing the fat into the flour.

Chilling dough Chill dough for 30 minutes before baking to prevent shrinkage.

A gentle touch The air can be pushed out of your dough by heavy or over-handling. Cut the fat up into small pieces before rubbing in, and then you won't need to handle the dough as much.

Cutting fat in Lard, hard margarine and butter can be used straight from the freezer if *grated* into the flour – thus benefiting the pastry with both coldness and those desired small pieces.

Flours for pastry Plain flour is the best to use for most pastries. As *air* is the chief constituent of successful pastry, you don't need the chemical raising agents of self-raising.

Fats for pastry Will vary according to pastry being made, but in general butter (best) and hard margarine give taste, while lard or cooking fat provide lightness. Many experts swear by a combination of the two.

Water Just as important, because too much will make dough soggy, too little and it won't roll.

Shortcrust Never add too much water. A rough guide is 1 teaspoon water to each 1 oz (25 g) flour or 3 good tablespoons to 8 oz (225 g).

Rich shortcrust Use a higher proportion of butter to flour (more than the usual half fat to flour), and an egg yolk in place of some water.

Puff Make with equal quantities of butter to (strong) flour, and butter must be of right consistency – not too soft and not too hard!

Even puff layers When rolling out, keep corners of the dough square and even, and then the layers will rise evenly.

Quiches and flans For crisp pastry underneath, bake the pastry case blind before adding filling. This ensures the pastry is thoroughly cooked. A flan case should also be placed on a hot baking sheet – which gives a more consistent heat under the tin than the oven shelves would.

Glazing pastry Never egg glaze any *cut* edges as the egg will coagulate and the pastry will not rise at that point – fatal for vol au vents.

What went wrong in general?

Soggy pastry	Made with too much water.
	No slit or hole in top to allow steam to escape.
	Pastry put on top of hot filling.
Uneven rising	Uneven rolling and no chilling.
Blisters on top	Uneven mixing of water.

What went wrong with shortcrust?

Hard and tough	Too much liquid, and probably over-baked.
Crumbly and difficult to handle	Too little water.
Pale on top, not cooked underneath	Too low in oven, not baked long enough.

What went wrong with puff?

Outside crisp, inside heavy and damp	Too hot an oven, so outside cooked too soon.
	Pastry rolled too thick.
Pastry shrinking from sides	Stretched during rolling, not allowed to rest in fridge before baking.

Better bread

Bread is another thing which, like pastry, is viewed with horror by many cooks. Basically, though, once you've got the hang of it, it's easy, much more economical – and such fun!

Fresh yeast It should not be creamed with sugar as a high concentration of sugar kills some of the yeast cells which causes the yeasty flavour of some home-made bread. Sugar is best mixed with dry ingredients, and yeast with water.

Storing fresh yeast Store in a loosely tied poly bag. It will keep for 4–5 days in a cold place, up to 1 month in the fridge, and up to 2 months in the freezer.

To test freshness of dried yeast Put dried yeast in a measure with a teaspoon of sugar and the amount of hand-hot water needed in the recipe. Whisk for a moment with a fork. If after 15 minutes it doesn't have a frothy head, then throw away, and buy some more.

White flour Strong white flour is easily the best for white loaves as it contains more stretchy gluten. But plain flour can work almost as well.

Wholemeal or wholewheat flour This contains the bran and the wheatgerm, as it is milled from the whole grain, with nothing taken out. This makes the healthiest brown bread. (A little added white flour makes it a little less solid.)

Wheatmeal flour This is a mixture of white and wholewheat, and gives a lighter textured loaf.

To speed up bread-making Warm the flour in a slow oven for a few minutes before mixing dough.

Other essentials Salt is necessary for flavour, and it strengthens the gluten in the flour. White fat or lard isn't vital, but helps to make bread lighter and keep longer. The liquid – usually water – should be lukewarm to encourage growth of yeast (too hot and it will kill the yeast). Mix 1/3 boiling water with 2/3 cold for a rough guide.

Kneading This develops the gluten in the flour which gives the dough its elasticity. It also strengthens the dough and spreads the yeast evenly. Knead until dough is smooth, slightly shiny, and feels firm and elastic.

Rising Always cover dough well during rising to prevent a skin forming on the surface. Use a lightly oiled poly bag or oiled clingfilm, or a large oiled plastic icecream container with a lid does the job perfectly.

Warm bread tins before use A warm dough placed in a cold tin for a second proving tends to give uneven rising of the dough. Best to warm tins a little in the oven first.

The oven This must be very hot initially, to kill the yeast. Bake for about 10 minutes at a very high heat, then lower temperature for remainder of cooking time (from approx 450°F/230°C/Gas 8 to 375°F/190°C/Gas 5).

Encourage crustiness Create steam by putting a roasting tin of boiling water on floor of oven.

Cooling bread Use a wire rack, as if left in tins, crust will be tough and bread soggy.

Non-stick bread Always brush tins with melted lard so the bread will turn out easily once cooked.

Freezing home-made bread It's as easy to make 3 or 4 loaves as it is to make 1, so batch bake. White bread and rolls with soft floury crusts, wholemeal and wheatmeal loaves freeze well.

Re-crisping loaves Bake in a hot oven at 450°F/240°C/Gas 8 for 8–10 minutes.

Common faults in bread-making

Poor volume and close texture	Under-proved. Too much salt. Oven too cool.
Uneven texture and holes	Too much yeast. Proved for too long.
Yeasty flavour	Too much yeast. Yeast creamed with sugar.

65

Cakes

I enjoy making cakes, and my family enjoy eating them. Many people are put off by what they believe are fiddly and time-consuming jobs – creaming butter and sugar, lining tins etc – but really cake-making is one of life's greatest pleasures!

Following the recipe This is *the* area of cooking where following a recipe *exactly* is a must. A little too much baking powder, for instance, and the texture of the cake will coarsen, or the top will crack.

Oven temperatures These too are vital for cake-making. If you haven't a thermometer (and they are *much* cheaper than asking an engineer to visit and test your thermostat), *always* notice whether your cake takes a longer or shorter time to cook than the recipe suggests, make a note of it, and adjust the cooker the next time.

Lining tins When cutting out greaseproof paper, cut several thicknesses at once – for spares.

Weighing ingredients For ease and speed, don't necessarily weigh out ingredients in order of recipe, but in order of stickiness! For instance, weigh flour, sugar etc first, *then* the butter, treacle etc, so that you don't have to keep washing the weighing pan.

All-in-one cakes The easiest method of all, and it also saves on washing up! Put everything in one bowl, and beat well. Use soft margarine which easily combines with the other ingredients. Because shorter beating time does not incorporate sufficient air, use baking powder as well as self-raising flour (1 level teaspoon to each 4 oz or 110 g of self-raising flour).

Mixing all-in-one cakes My mixer means making all-in-one cakes is simplicity itself, but to prevent flour scattering all over the floor, 1 cover the front end of the machine and the bowl with a teatowel (watch carefully to see towel doesn't slip and get caught in the spindle).

Sandwich sponge cakes the same size? To be certain that both cake tins have an equal amount of mixture, weigh tins filled with the mixture, and balance quantity so both tins weigh the same.

Tray bakes This is the fastest way of making cakes. Line a meat tin with foil, grease it, and use to bake the mixture in. Ice in the tin when baked so there are no drips of icing, and slice into squares or fingers.

Bake without delay Bake whisked sponge cakes immediately, as they won't produce good results if allowed to stand before baking.

How to tell when a cake is done A Victoria sandwich should shrink slightly from the sides of the tin, and top should spring back after being pressed lightly. Test a fruit cake with a fine metal skewer; if it comes out clean cake is done.

Slightly sinking cake If you notice a fruit or Madeira cake has a slight dip in the centre when it comes out of the oven, turn out onto greaseproof paper on a wire tray *upside down*. The weight of the cake cooling will make top level.

Disastrously sunken cake Cut out the centre and fill with fruit and whipped cream. If it is fruit cake, take out centre carefully and cut slices around cake. Serve arranged on a plate.

Before icing Spread cake with apricot jam, as this prevents icing going into the cake (especially good with chocolate cakes). Warm the jam first – with sponge fillings too – as it then spreads easily and will not tear top of cake.

To make icing set more quickly Mix icing sugar for water icing with a little boiling water.

To coat sides of cake unstickily First brush sides with apricot jam then put the chopped nuts, chocolate vermicelli or grated chocolate on a sheet of greaseproof paper. Hold the cake by top and bottom and roll in decoration until sides are evenly coated.

Biscuits, scones, pancakes etc

People often apologise for offering biscuits instead of cakes to their tea-time guests. I cannot think why, as a real home-made biscuit is one of the most mouth-watering of delicacies. They are also quick to make on the whole, as are scones and pancakes – and as they can be frozen, they are good for emergencies.

Tastier biscuits Make – if appropriate to the finished result – with sugar which has had a vanilla pod stored in it.

Thinner biscuits Many soft and thin biscuits change shape as you move them onto baking sheets. Roll them out instead *on* a greased baking sheet (one without a lip, or the *back* of one with a lip), and cut out. Remove dough between biscuits, and bake tray as is.

Fast biscuits Shape dough into a sausage, wrap in clingfilm and chill for about 1 hour. Slice into thin circles and bake in the usual way.

Shaping biscuits Another quick way is to chill dough, then roll into walnut-sized balls on a greased baking sheet. Butter the bottom of a glass and press onto each 'walnut' in turn to flatten. Sugar glass bottom too if appropriate.

Preparing baking sheets Most biscuits should be baked on greased baking sheets, but always follow the recipe instructions. Mixtures containing syrup, treacle, oatmeal or cheese, for instance, will be better baked on ungreased baking sheets that have been sprinkled with flour.

To see when biscuits are done Run a knife underneath and lift up so that you can see the bottom as well as the top. If the ones on the outside are done before those in the middle, lift onto a cooling tray and return others to the oven.

To see when scones are done They should be well risen, golden brown, and done underneath. Break one in half to check the inside.

Stale-ish scones? If left over, why not cut them in half, and toast for breakfast. Delicious with marmalade, like toast, or with a fried egg on top, accompanied by a rasher of bacon.

Cooling biscuits Many biscuits should be transferred straightaway to a wire rack to cool and harden. But many are too soft after baking to be moved immediately, especially those made with syrup or honey, so must be left on sheets for a few moments to harden.

Don't overlap biscuits while cooling Many will bend and become misshapen as they cool and harden on the rack.

Storing biscuits Never store in the same tin as cake as the biscuits will absorb moisture from the cake and become soft.

Re-crisping biscuits If the biscuit tin lid has been left off, put the soft biscuits on a baking sheet in a moderate oven for about 5 minutes. Remove from the oven, cool and they crisp again. Don't turn the oven on specially, just pop them in after cooking something else.

Delicious crunchy shortbread For a coarser texture, use half rice flour or semolina to flour.

To vary your shortbread recipe Pipe mixture into shapes on a tray rather than baking in tin. In rounds, you can top with jam; fingers can be dipped in melted chocolate; and you can add grated lemon rind, glacé cherries or chopped walnuts too.

Drop scones The correct consistency of the batter is *vital*. It should be thick enough for the mixture when dropped from the spoon to gradually disappear. If too thick, the scones will be uncooked in the middle, and if too thin, won't rise properly.

Cooling drop scones The instruction to cool drop scones in a clean cloth or teatowel is important to their ultimate texture. This traps the steam, keeping them soft and springy.

Freezing scones and pancakes Open-freeze uncooked scones, and then pack in a poly bag. Thaw and bake, and you've got instant tea! Interleave pancakes with greaseproof or foil for the freezer so that you can separate them easily for reheating.

Success with sauces

Sauces of all kinds – especially if made with the best ingredients: butter instead of margarine, a béchamel milk (see below) or a good stock – are a wonderful way of enhancing foods, easing their digestion, complementing them. The simplest dish can be transformed into a feast with the addition of a good sauce.

Stock in sauces Needless to say, if making a brown or velouté sauce, a good flavoursome and related stock – chicken for chicken dishes, veal for veal dishes – will be the best.

Milk in sauces Instead of plain milk, a 'béchamel' milk adds incomparable flavour to many white sauces. Put ½ pt (300 ml) milk in a pan with a small piece of onion or a sliced shallot, a bay leaf, a clove, and a few white peppercorns. Bring *slowly* to the boil to extract maximum flavours, then set aside, off heat, cover, and infuse for 10–15 minutes. Strain and use hot or cold, to make a sauce.

Making gravy This originally meant the natural juices which came out of a roast, but now applies to a sauce made from them – usually in the tin in which the roast was cooked. Strain off fat carefully, leaving behind the sediment, juices and crispy brown bits which will be the heart of the gravy. Sprinkle flour into the tin, and stir briskly, getting all bits up, and then add stock or water in which vegetables were cooked. Bring to the boil, then taste and season, and simmer until correct consistency (usually thick for a stuffed roast, thin for all others, but it's a matter of personal taste).

If gravy goes lumpy This often happens when flour is added to pan. Try mixing flour to a paste with a little water in a cup, then stirring in some stock, *then* pouring into the pan. Be sure to stir all goodness from pan into gravy, and you may need some browning to get correct colour.

If sauce goes lumpy Remove from heat and whisk in processor until smooth, or sieve.

To avoid lumps in sauce When bringing to the boil, stir all the time so that it thickens evenly. A wire whisk – a special small one for sauces – will be much better than a wooden spoon.

Clear sauces Use arrowroot for really clear sauces, as it becomes transparent when cooked. Cornflour does, too, to a lesser extent.

Stop sauces curdling Do not boil a sauce which contains cream or an egg yolk. If it becomes too hot it will curdle.

Glossy sauces If a white sauce lacks gloss it is because of lack of cooking after liquid was added. Return to the heat, bring to the boil and simmer for 2 minutes, beating well all the time.

To enrich sauces When sauce is fully cooked, an added egg yolk will further thicken it and give it a gloss. Add a little sauce to yolk in a cup, mix and *then* stir mixture back into the sauce, off the heat.

Make in advance Put a piece of damp greaseproof or butter paper on top to stop skin forming.

Keeping sauces hot Keep prepared sauces hot without catching by standing the pan in a larger pan filled with hot water – or a bain marie – so that the base of the pan isn't in direct contact with the heat.

Thinning or thickening sauces The former is easy, by just adding extra stock, milk or perhaps cream, but the latter is more difficult. You may have to cook down, to reduce it by evaporation, or you could add an egg yolk and cream (*don't* boil). Beurre manié works well: mash together with a fork equal amounts of butter and flour, and drop small balls of it one at a time into the sauce. Whisk it continually to blend, then boil for a minute or so to cook the flour.

Sauces in the blender Many – even the most complicated oil and egg-yolk sauces like mayonnaise, and butter and egg-yolk sauces like hollandaise – can be made in the blender. Follow the recipe instructions very carefully – it saves so much time!

Leftover sauces Never throw them away. Use in soups, add other ingredients to stuff veg or pancakes, or use with garnishes on canapés.

Herbs and spices

Used carefully, both herbs and spices can add flavour, character and subtlety to dishes better than anything else. Both, too, have been known for centuries for their preservative and health-giving properties.

Grow your own herbs For almost instant access to a herb as required, grow them in a small plot in the garden – one plant of each will probably meet most families' requirements. If no room in the garden, parsley and chives, and many other herbs, will grow happily in a sunny windowbox or in pots on a windowsill in the kitchen where they will be near to hand.

Storing fresh herbs Wrap them separately in paper towels then put in plastic bags in the vegetable drawer of the fridge.

Harvesting herbs for drying Pick leaves when flowers are just in bud. Harvest flowers just before fully open. Seeds should be gathered when heads turn brown and seeds rattle loose.

Drying herbs Most herbs can be tied in small bunches, and hung upside down by the stems in a cool, dark airy place – a loft or spare room. They will dry within about 2–3 weeks. When brittle, strip leaves from stems and store in airtight opaque containers.

Drying herbs in the microwave Choose the leafy herbs like parsley, basil and tarragon. Remove all stalks and place leaves on kitchen paper in the microwave. Dry on low power until crisp.

Freezing herbs A good way of retaining fresh flavour is to mix chopped leafy herbs with softened butter. Roll into a sausage, wrap, seal and label, then freeze. Add a slice of the herb butter straight to soups and stews, or use slices to top fish, steaks or chops.

To 'chop' frozen herbs Crumble them up in the bag in which they were frozen by rubbing bag between your hands. Or, if in a block, by rubbing against side of coarse grater.

Herby ice cubes Make ice cubes in normal way, and insert a herb sprig – good for drinks, but wonderful for a cold summer soup, for instance.

Make herb vinegars Easy, and so much more interesting in cooking or in salad dressings. Use 1 pt (550 ml) of loosely packed leaves and cover with the same volume of white wine vinegar. Close jar or bottle and leave for 2-3 weeks to allow the flavour to develop.

Leftover freshly chopped parsley Keep for several days in the fridge in a screw-top jar with holes in the lid. Useful for garnishes.

Parsley stalks Most of the flavour is in them – and most of the goodness – so add them to stocks, soups and stews. Remove before serving.

Buying spices Buy whole if possible (now commonly available in ethnic shops, delis and better food stores), and in the smallest quantity.

Storing spices Whole spices keep freshest, stored in tightly lidded jars in a cool dark place. Ground, they last less long.

Grinding spices If grinding in quantity – to make garam masala for curries, for instance – use a coffee grinder. A mortar and pestle is invaluable for smaller quantities. And most hand-held graters have a surface reserved for nutmeg.

Herbs and spices in casseroles and stews Put herbs, peppercorns, mace and bay leaf into a tea infuser in a casserole. All the flavour comes through the holes and there are no bits to fish out when the dish is cooled. (This is also a good way of enjoying a herbal or spicy bath; all the herbs or spices are contained, so don't mess up the bath water!)

Spice up your life Even if not cooking exotic, spicy international dishes, spices can contribute to your cooking. The smallest amount can make a great difference. Add a touch of nutmeg to rice puddings, to steamed spinach, to white sauces; add ground cinnamon to kebab marinades or use whole as a swizzle stick for hot chocolate; add some ground cloves to Christmas pudding mixes or to apple dishes.

Breath sweeteners Chewing parsley neutralises the odour of garlic or onion; cloves do too.

Problems with preserving

There should be none, as preserving is basically one of the most simple and satisfying of home skills – it takes little more than time and patience to produce a delicious range of jams, chutneys and pickles.

Setting test for preserves Use a thermometer to 212°F/100°C, or spoon a small amount onto a cold saucer. When it has cooled, the skin that forms should wrinkle when pushed with a finger.

Sugar for jam Warm it in the oven whilst cooking the fruit, as this speeds up the dissolving process when fruit and sugar are mixed together.

Jam jars Use clear glass jars, and warm them before filling with hot jam – by putting in very low oven, or soaking in hot water – to ensure that they won't crack.

Tops for jam jars Cut circles out of waxed paper from cereal boxes. Saves buying special discs. Remember to have handy a good supply of rubber bands!

Lids for chutneys They must be vinegar-proof. Use plastic-coated screw-on lids or vinegar-proof plastic sheet. Cellophane covers let the vinegar evaporate as they are not completely airtight, and therefore the chutney shrinks.

Chutney storage Most home-made chutneys should be stored for a couple of months before eating to allow flavours time to develop and mature.

Jam storage Best kept in a dry, cool dark place. Heat makes the contents shrink, light can fade the colour, and damp may cause mould to grow on the surface of the jam. Check stock occasionally.

Sugary jam If an opened jar of jam or honey has gone hard and sugary, stand jar in a pan of water and heat gently until sugariness disappears.

Drinks from jelly pulp A good home-made concentrated drink can be made by boiling up pulp from jelly-making with water and sugar. Strain and dilute to taste. Apple and blackberry is delicious.

Jam problems

Does not set

The fruit may have been over-ripe or damp.

Insufficient pectin in the fruit. More can be added – a fruit high in pectin like apple or gooseberries – but the flavour will suffer.

Setting point may have been reached, and the jam allowed to boil *on*.

Jam is scorched

The base of the preserving pan was not heavy enough.

Jam lacks flavour

Probably over-boiled – which also makes it stiff.

Fruit is tough

Sugar may have been added before skin/peel was tender.

Fruit will toughen, rather than soften, when sugar is added.

Jam ferments

Over-ripe fruit was used, or too little sugar.

Jam goes mouldy

The seal of the bottle may have broken, or damp fruit was used.

Bottling problems

Fruit rises in bottles

Water in water bath has been heated too rapidly.

Occurs particularly when syrup is heavy.

Poor flavour/colour

May be due to over-cooking or to unripe fruit.

Fruit fermenting

May be due to over-ripe fruit or insufficient sterilising of bottles.

Mould

May be caused by insufficient sterilising or by poor seal. If seal found to be defective after bottles and contents have cooked, it is possible to rectify, by re-processing, but quality will be impaired.

Chutney problems

Muddy appearance

May be due to use of ground spices (instead of bruised whole spices, tied in muslin bag).

Children in the kitchen

The kitchen is often the centre of the house where mother or father – thus the children too – spend a lot of their time. It can be a place of fascination, as children are keen from a very early age to 'help' with preparation, washing up and cooking, but it can also be a place of quite considerable danger.

Safety in the kitchen This is paramount if you have small children. You will have chosen your cooker or hob for its dials and plates set back from the edge; poisonous or dangerous substances – bleach, white spirit, even aspirin if you keep it in the kitchen – will be in a locked or inaccessible (wall-mounted, perhaps) cupboard; and all electric floor points should have some sort of guard on them.

Cupboard safety clips A cheaper solution (for children *do* grow up quite quickly) is to sticky-tape doors shut. Tape is also useful to carry with you when you visit childless households.

Pan handles Get into the habit of always, while cooking, turning the handles inwards, so that a child cannot grab at them.

Sharp knives These should never be in drawers – store them out of reach at the back of working surfaces.

First-aid kit The most basic one, which should be in every kitchen, consists of: plain white gauze, assorted roller bandages and adhesive dressings, adhesive sticking plaster, a polythene bowl and sterile cotton wool balls (for minor cuts); assorted sizes of prepared sterile dressings (for bandaging wounds); safety pins (often easier than tying); scissors; antihistamine cream (for bites and stings); Paracetamol tablets (better than aspirin); and a thermometer.

Burns and scalds The commonest accident in the kitchen, and the best treatment is always dousing in cold water. Hold burned area under cold running water, and always with a child, if burn is larger than his hand, see the doctor.

Helping hands Make sure they are clean first. Insist on an apron, and encourage cleaning up as they go along.

Help with the housework Make fun dusters by drawing or

embroidering faces on old white socks. They won't mind the odd chore if it is fun to do.

Washing up The smallest toddler can help with this if the water isn't too hot, you oversee, and don't let him near your best glasses!

Preparing vegetables A healthy way of introducing children to 'cooking'. They can string beans, peel potatoes, scrub potatoes and carrots, 'peel' cooked beetroot, and remove leaves from sprouts.

Grating cheese Turning the handle of a Mouli-type cheese mill is fun for most children.

Allocate a job A child will enjoy food if he has helped prepare it. Even potentially hazardous jobs can have his collaboration: he could smear a chop with mustard, prick the sausages, arrange things in a baking tin, or even dip fish or meat in a coating batter.

Dividing kitchen chores For older children, draw up a chart giving each child different chores each day – this minimises arguments and makes sure that everyone gets their share of the 'preferred' or 'hated' tasks.

Working in the kitchen Always supervise and *advise* in the kitchen – on use of sharp knives (always on a wooden board), for instance, and about not putting hot pans on a working surface without a mat.

Leftover pastry Save oddments for children to cut into novelty shapes or to make into jam or savoury tartlets. If fine, let them do it on a board in the garden, then there's no mess!

Choosing what to cook Something they enjoy eating, or something they can be given as a present. My children enjoy making pizzas, dips and sausage rolls, and icecream, cakes and popcorn.

Packed lunches

As the quality of school lunches and snack bars can sometimes leave a lot to be desired, a good and healthful packed lunch is often the answer for both children and working adults.

Balancing the 'menu' Just as at home, packed lunches require forethought. Have a balance of protein, carbohydrate and some fresh fruit or vegetables. Offer a contrast of textures and of colours, and a drink of some sort as well. If something sweet is demanded, dried fruit and nuts are healthier than confectionery.

Packed lunch necessities To avoid scattered rubbish, include a polythene bag in which peel, crusts etc can be either disposed of or brought home. Some paper tissues for napkins or a packeted wipe would be useful too.

Salt and pepper Special picnic containers are available, but they often fall apart. A very handy dispenser is a paper drinking straw! Twist one end, fill with salt and pepper, then twist the other end closed.

Crudités for health Fill a small polythene bag with cucumber fingers, carrot and celery sticks, cauliflower florets and radishes.

Have a dip Make up your favourite recipe – from cream cheese or avocados, or buy or make humus or taramasalata – and enclose in a small yogurt or cream pot, covered with clingfilm, for dipping crudités into.

Dip into a pâté Or make this pâté. Blend 1 lb (450 g) chicken livers with 8 oz (225 g) softened butter and 4 tablespoons brandy. Cook in individual ramekin dishes in a bain marie at 325°F/160°C/Gas 3 for 30 minutes. Pack one per lunchbox, and freeze any remaining for another day. This ought perhaps to be for adults only!

Pitta bread special An unusual sandwich. Split the pitta bread and lightly butter inside. Fill with a cold omelette. Add tomato and cucumber slices too if you like. Wrap in clingfilm.

Real French bread sandwiches Just like you would find in a French charcuterie. Take lengths of French bread and slice across at angles but *not* right through, then fill the cuts with fillings; sliced tomato

78

and chopped spring onion; sliced hard-boiled egg, mayonnaise and chopped chives; slivers of Brie; a mixture of walnuts, apple, celery and mayonnaise.

American double deckers For good appetites, sandwich 3 slices of bread together (brown *and* white), and fill with: cheese and chive; tomato, cucumber, watercress; fish or meat and salad.

Avoiding butter Peanut butter or cream cheese can be spread instead; try redcurrant jelly for a lamb sandwich, or a mild mustard with beef.

Buttering sandwiches Keep butter at room temperature so that it is easy to spread, and spread right to the edge of each slice of bread. This will prevent moist fillings like tomato making the bread go soggy.

Easy-to-slice bread Best fresh, and chilled in the fridge. Butter *before* slicing.

Use up breadcrumbs Don't waste the soft bread scooped out of loaves and rolls. Freeze, and then make into stuffings and bread sauce.

Preparing in advance Wrap sandwiches with foil, grease-proof paper or clingfilm. Most can be frozen – but not those with hard-boiled egg or salad. Pack in stacks of 6 or 8, interleaved with foil, and put an extra slice at each end.

Finger foods Don't forget protein foods like chunks of cheese, chicken legs, peppercorn sausages, individual quiches (bake in patty or Yorkshire pudding tins), slices of a larger quiche or pie, or hard-boiled eggs.

Fruit and nut cases Tuck small bags of peanuts, raisins and dried fruit into a lunchbox.

Add some fruit Apples, bananas and other fruit come in their own wrappings – but a peeled orange wrapped in clingfilm saves lunchtime bother.

Super soups Small vacuum flasks are now available for cold days and hot soups. Avoid soups containing milk or cream; they don't keep well.

Washing up

A chore most cooks hate, but if you're organised properly, sink washing up shouldn't be too horrific. And if you've got a dishwasher, all you've really got to do is stack it!

Wash to order Always wash in the following order; glasses first, followed by silver, cutlery, non-greasy plates and dishes, greasy china and dishes, then the cooking pans last. Stack them for washing in this order too.

First things first Fill oven dishes, pie dishes, messy pans etc with hand-hot water with a squirt of washing-up liquid. Leave to one side. (If you greased the dishes properly before use, you shouldn't find cleaning too terrible.)

Cold water soaks Hot water will cook and fix egg and uncooked flour – batter, for instance, or a blend of flour and water in a bowl – so soak in *cold* water.

Washing cups Always try to wash separately as handles can easily be broken off in a crowded bowl.

Cutlery Stand all cutlery, handles upwards (to protect bone, wood, china etc), in a jug of hand-hot soapy water or maybe a lightly soiled pan, and soak for a while before washing.

Washing sharp knives or processor blades Never leave in a bowl of dirty washing-up water. Best to slip knives into a tall jug of soapy water, and the blades into a separate small bowl.

Washing plates After scraping clean (use a plastic spatula or similar to scrape off encrustations), *float* down separately into hot water so that each surface is wetted.

Cleaning crystal or cut glass Wash as you would ordinary glass, but scrub the indentations with a soft nail brush to clean thoroughly.

Cleaning a decanter Rinse as soon as possible after use to avoid staining, but if too late, fill with warm water and an abrasive of some kind like sand (butlers used to use lead shot). Shake hard and leave to stand. Rinse well.

Cleaning encrusted forks Stab several times into a plastic net pan cleaner. Watch your hands!

Cleaning a vacuum flask Crush an eggshell and put inside with a little hot water. Shake vigorously for a few minutes, then rinse well.

Take care of your hands Try to wear rubber gloves when washing up. Once gloves have holes they can be used for dry, dirty jobs around the house and garden.

Double sink advantages You can wash up in one, and rinse in hot water in the other. This saves on drying as most glasses and plates will dry spotlessly clean after a good hot rinse.

Polishing glasses Use linen teatowels in preference to cotton as they absorb moisture, and are also less fluffy than cotton.

Plimsoll lines on cups Tea stains are easily rubbed off with scouring powder or salt.

Save on washing up Line grill trays with foil to catch drips when grilling bacon, chops etc. If foil gets too dirty, throw it away, saving the fat. Otherwise wipe the foil while still warm and re-use it.

Save time on drying Buy a second drainer and stand it in front of the first, or cover a table or other surface with a couple of teatowels to provide more drip-drying space.

Drying tins and trays A warm oven is the best place for thoroughly drying metal tins and trays. Be careful not to put plastic or wooden handles in the oven.

For extra safety Line a bowl or sink with a teatowel for special china, and put a foam rubber mat under drainer.

Separate washing When there's a baby in the house, or if someone has a cold, wash all utensils separately. The same goes for pet dishes.

Laundry time

Like washing up, this is something that just can't be avoided. The advent of modern washing machines, spin-driers, and tumble driers has revolutionised the old Monday washing-day blues, but many fabrics and problems still have to be dealt with by hand.

Choosing a washing machine Important considerations are size and where it is to be sited – have you room in the kitchen? – and enough wash programmes for your needs. Does the load weight correspond to your family's wash? Does it spin-dry well enough to iron and, if it has a tumble drier incorporated, does it have an anti-crease device?

Automatics They are less economical to run than twin tubs, but save time. They use more energy and water than twin tubs, but one with a cold water fill as well as a hot water fill will save money (many clothes don't really *need* to be washed in hot water).

Choosing a tumble drier Many can fit on top of or beside a washing machine, thus saving space. One with both a hot and cold tumble is best, as some clothes cannot stand heat. Some also need an exterior outlet, so position carefully.

Wash symbols These are a boon for all washers, but must be followed meticulously.

The article can be washed by machine or hand. Figure above water line tells which wash process and that below the water temperature, °C.

– Hand wash only.

– Do not wash at all.

– Do not dry clean.

– Indicates the ironing process. Dots indicate temperature: 1 = cool, 2 = warm; 3 = hot. A cross through iron means do not iron.

– Tumble drying recommended. A cross through means do not tumble dry.

Stain removal A box or kit of proprietary stain-removers handy in the kitchen is useful for emergencies, but the essence of all stain removal is *speed*. Act quickly, and if article can be soaked, do so in lots of cold water. If cold doesn't work, try lukewarm water with ordinary soap. Never use hot water as this can *set* stains.

If you give up If soaking and branded cleaners don't work, take your stain to the dry cleaner. Point the stain out, say what you think it is, and hopefully they can solve your problem.

Test for colour fastness If unsure, wet a corner and squeeze it in a white towel.

Whites and coloureds A cliché, but ought to be repeated: never wash pale fabrics with darker fabrics. However fast you think they might be, it's not worth the risk.

Boiling clothes Useful for getting out stains which ordinary washing leaves behind. It sterilises as well, so is useful for hankies, nappies, teatowels, face cloths and dish cloths.

Drying washing outside Always remember to wash the line and stand with your back to the wind so that wet clothes do not flap in your face. Peg the tails and bottoms of shirts so that wind can blow up sleeves.

Cleaning pegs These cause many of the stains on clothes if dirty, so keep them in a separate bag free from dust, with strings to go over one arm so that you can reach in to the bag with the other hand.

Saving soap Save odds and ends of soap, as they can be grated on your hand grater to make your very own soap 'flakes' for hand washing.

Ironing damp This is best for many clothes. Roll them up to keep damp longer. Silk *needs* to be thus ironed, and if you can't iron straightaway, pop in a plastic bag damp, and store in fridge! Always remember to air, though, after ironing.

Ironing board Buy one without an asbestos mat to hold the iron. Many irons can clog up with the fibres, and there are fears that the tiny amount of dust involved can be dangerous.

Tricky and miscellaneous things

In this section I've slotted all the tips that didn't seem to fit naturally anywhere else, and they range from removing stains from wallpapers to polishing windows with my own special method!

The cleaning box To save time and energy, I always carry all the equipment needed to clean throughout the house in a large handled box. I store in it: brush and dustpan, furniture and floor polish, turpentine or white spirit, dusters, bleach, scouring powder, a couple of damp J-cloths, a cream cleaner, floor cleaner, and disinfectant. If I could fit the broom and vacuum cleaner in too, I would!

Removing cobwebs Wrap a duster over the head of the broom to reach for cobwebs, dirt on top of picture rails and tops of windows.

Cleaning white surfaces Use a mixture of bicarbonate of soda, bleach and water for sinks, tiles, paintwork etc.

Grease spots on wallpaper Place a piece of blotting paper over stain and iron over with a warm iron.

A clean telephone Remove grease and dirt with a little methylated spirit on a cloth.

Cleaning windows I've used all brands of window-cleaning agents – the best is my own. Simply take a plastic garden spray or laundry spray bottle, and fill with 1 part ammonia to 3 parts water. Spray lightly over window, then rub over with kitchen paper on top of a pad of soft cloth, then add another sheet of kitchen paper to polish off. Use this to clean the next window, then add another fresh sheet to polish. Uses a lot of kitchen roll, and the smell is pretty horrid, but it works wonders.

Cleaning Venetian blinds Put on a pair of old fabric gloves. Dip fingers into warm soapy water and draw each slat through the fingers to remove grime.

To clean oven Dissolve 1 tablespoon caustic soda in ½ pt (300 ml) hot water. Separately, mix 1 tablespoon flour and a little water to a thick paste and add this to the soda solution. Mix and bottle. Apply to cooker on a pad, using rubber gloves. Do not spill, and do not get too near. Do not use on self-cleaning surfaces.

To clean oven shelves Soak in a deep sink of hot water with added biological and enzyme washing powder. Use for the grill pan as well. If unsuccessful, scrape with wire wool, but do wear rubber gloves for your fingers' sake.

Cleaning marble Paint the surface with a mixture of 1 part powdered pumice, 1 part powdered chalk and 2 parts bicarbonate of soda. Leave on for at least a day, then wash off with clean water and a firm sponge.

Cracks in lino Can be repaired by using sticky tape protected by a coat of polyurethane clear varnish.

To polish lino Put 1 tablespoon paraffin into 1 pt (550 ml) warm water. Wash floor to give a shine without making floor slippery.

To clean brass Mix lemon juice with Brasso to keep it brighter longer. A very dirty piece of brass can be cleaned by leaving it in Coca-Cola overnight! (A frightening thought!)

To clean copper Clean with salt and vinegar, or ½ lemon dipped in salt. Rinse well then polish.

Tarnished silver If forks or spoons have been tarnished by egg, for instance, put in an aluminium pan with 1 pt (550 ml) water and 2 tablespoons washing soda. Bring to the boil and leave forks and spoons in for 5 minutes until black stain has gone. Silver dip works well too.

Squeaking door Oil the hinges with sewing-machine, bicycle, or 3-in-1 oil. Use a feather or small brush to drip it in – it works like magic.

Smooth-running drawers Old-fashioned drawers often stick after years of use. Rub the top and bottom edges with beeswax or a candle.

Separating glasses To separate stuck-together glasses, stand both in warm water and fill the top one with cold water – it worked for me!

Index

A selection of bestsellers from SPHERE

FICTION

HOOLIGANS	William Diehl	£2.75 ☐
UNTO THIS HOUR	Tom Wicker	£2.95 ☐
ORIENTAL HOTEL	Janet Tanner	£2.50 ☐
CATACLYSM	William Clark	£2.50 ☐
THE GOLDEN EXPRESS	Derek Lambert	£2.25 ☐

FILM AND TV TIE-INS

SANTA CLAUS THE NOVEL	£1.75 ☐
SANTA CLAUS STORYBOOK	£2.50 ☐
SANTA CLAUS JUMBO COLOURING BOOK	£1.25 ☐
SANTA CLAUS: THE BOY WHO DIDN'T BELIEVE IN CHRISTMAS	£1.50 ☐
SANTA CLAUS: SIMPLE PICTURES TO COLOUR	95p ☐

NON-FICTION

HORROCKS	Philip Warner	£2.95 ☐
1939 THE WORLD WE LEFT BEHIND	Robert Kee	£4.95 ☐
BUMF	Alan Coren	£1.75 ☐
I HATE SEX		£0.99 ☐
BYE BYE CRUEL WORLD	Tony Husband	£1.25 ☐

All Sphere books are available at your local bookshop or newsagent, or can be ordered direct from the publisher. Just tick the titles you want and fill in the form below.

Name _____

Address _____

_____

Write to Sphere Books, Cash Sales Department, P.O. Box 11, Falmouth, Cornwall TR10 9EN

Please enclose a cheque or postal order to the value of the cover price plus:

UK: 45p for the first book, 20p for the second book and 14p for each additional book ordered to a maximum charge of £1.63.

OVERSEAS: 75p for the first book plus 21p per copy for each additional book.

BFPO & EIRE: 45p for the first book, 20p for the second book plus 14p per copy for the next 7 books, thereafter 8p per book.

Sphere Books reserve the right to show new retail prices on covers which may differ from those previously advertised in the text or elsewhere, and to increase postal rates in accordance with the PO.